TELL OUR STORY

TELL OUR STORY

MULTIPLYING VOICES IN THE NEWS MEDIA

JULIE REID AND DALE T. MCKINLEY

WITS UNIVERSITY PRESS

Published in South Africa by:
Wits University Press
1 Jan Smuts Avenue
Johannesburg 2001

www.witspress.co.za

First published 2020

http://dx.doi.org.10.18772/22020055775

978-1-77614-577-5 (Paperback)
978-1-77614-581-2 (Hardback)
978-1-77614-578-2 (Web PDF)
978-1-77614-579-9 (EPUB)
978-1-77614-580-5 (Mobi)

Project manager: Catherine Damerell
Copyeditor: Sally Hines
Proofreader: Alison Lockhart
Indexer: Tessa Botha
Cover design: Hybrid Creative
Typeset in 10 point Minion Pro

CONTENTS

LIST OF FIGURES

ACKNOWLEDGEMENTS

We are grateful to the Open Society Foundation of South Africa, and the Women in Research Fund, awarded by the University of South Africa (UNISA), for providing the funding that made the research for this book possible.

This research was conducted under the auspices of the Media Policy and Democracy Project (MPDP). We are additionally grateful for the guidance and advice provided by fellow MPDP researchers, in particular the project leaders, Professor Jane Duncan (University of Johannesburg) and Professor Viola Milton (UNISA), who were extremely helpful in fundraising for this project.

Our thanks extend to Taryn Isaacs De Vega (Rhodes University) for assisting us with the media content analysis, which is reported on in this book, and to Dr Vanessa Malila (Rhodes University) who transcribed the in-depth interviews.

But most especially, our sincere thanks is extended to the courageous and determined activists and residents of Glebelands, Thembelihle and Xolobeni/Amadiba,[1] who warmly welcomed us into their communities, fully supported and actively participated in this project, and without whom this book would not have been possible.

This book is dedicated to them.

ABBREVIATIONS AND ACRONYMS

ACC	Amadiba Crisis Committee
ANC	African National Congress
ANN7	African News Network 7
BCCSA	Broadcasting Complaints Commission of South Africa
COPE	Congress of the People
CSO	civil society organisation
EWN	Eyewitness News
GHCVV	Glebelands Hostel Community Violence Victims
IFP	Inkatha Freedom Party
MPDP	Media Policy and Democracy Project
MRC	Mineral Resource Commodities
PCSA	Press Council of South Africa
SABC	South African Broadcasting Corporation
SANRAL	South African National Roads Agency Limited
SAPS	South African Police Service
TCC	Thembelihle Crisis Committee
UK	United Kingdom
UNESCO	United Nations Educational, Scientific and Cultural Organization
UNISA	University of South Africa
XOLCO	Xolobeni Empowerment Company

1

The Importance of Voice and the Myth of the 'Voiceless'

Julie Reid

> Voice as a process – giving account of oneself and what affects
> one's life – is an irreducible part of what it means to be human;
> effective voice (the effective opportunity to have one's voice
> heard and taken into account) is a human good.
> — Nick Couldry, *Why Voice Matters*

As social animals, all human beings instinctively and naturally yearn to give an account of themselves and to tell their own stories. But, to operate as if certain peoples lack this desire or ability is to behave towards them as if they are not human (Couldry 2010). In recent years, philosophers and social scientists have pondered the notion of 'voice' as a type of catch-all phrase that infers more than the literal meaning of the word, that is, the sounds and words one makes when speaking. Jim Macnamara (2012) conceptualises 'voice' as more than the verbal act of speaking since it includes human communication of all types, such as voting, protesting, online participation and artistic production. More broadly, voice, or rather the ability to practise voice, relies on inclusion and participation in political, economic and social expression and processes, and involves affording people the space to actively contribute to decisions that affect their lives. Jo Tacchi (2008: 1) calls the denial of the right of peoples to participate in such activity, 'voice poverty'.

Voice today is theoretically understood to encompass a broad spectrum of communicative activity, which includes: iterating one's view, story and position in the world; having that story or position listened to by others; having one's story recognised as something that matters; and, further, having it mediated or carried via a means of communication (such as the news media) to the broader collective or society. Admittedly, that is putting things rather simply because there are complex and multi-layered problems and conditions relevant to each one of these steps. A number of writers examine the intricacies of this process, the notion of 'voice', its definition, its theorisation, its associated processes and, crucially, the characteristic challenges prevalent in the disablement of the effective practice of voice. Particularly notable among these is work done by Susan Bickford (1996), the research collective called the Listening Project (O'Donnell, Lloyd and Dreher 2009) and Nick Couldry (2009, 2010). Bickford (1996) offers a landmark and detailed examination of voice and associated listening in her book, *The Dissonance of Democracy: Listening, Conflict, and Citizenship*, in which she explores 'pathbuilding' communicative practices. Here, citizens engage with one another's perspectives through an ongoing process of speaking and listening, though not necessarily with the goal of social coherence. Instead, the discord, which naturally arises during these interactions, encourages participants to re-evaluate their own speaking practices (Bickford 1996).

Charles Husband (1996, 2008) amplifies the ethical importance of listening by advocating the 'right to be understood' as a fundamental communication right. Lisbeth Lipari (2010) proposes a paradigm shift that places listening at the centre of communication rather than speaking, and she defines a perspective on listening, which she calls 'listening being'. While the largest body of literature emphasises the notion of listening as central to communication, Couldry (2009, 2010) focuses the critical lens on voice. We take particular direction from his explication of the various characteristics of 'voice'. However, while he identifies a number of different levels of voice, we will mention only those that are relevant here in relation to how voice is either carried out or ignored by the dominant news media, and what the implications are for journalism.

While the body of scholarly literature on communicative voice and listening, and the associated ethics involved, is steadily growing, we do not offer a detailed literature review of such writings here because this has already been presented at length elsewhere (see, for example, Dreher 2009, 2017; Macnamara 2012; O'Donnell 2009; O'Donnell, Lloyd and Dreher 2009). Rather, what we offer in this book is a demonstration of such theory in practice: we intend this as an example of active listening, with the purpose of surfacing and amplifying voice as a means to illustrate how this could be translated into journalistic practice for application in the news media.

In this book, we have kept the theoretical side of things unapologetically simple. This is because, with respect to our scholarly peers, we do not want the journalists, future journalists-in-training, newsmakers and editors who read this book to become discouraged by complexities and near-unfathomable musings so characteristic of academic writing (Heleta 2016). Rather, we adopt the principled position of offering a text that is easy to read, easy to understand and more broadly accessible, knowing that this approach offers greater potential to catalyse the type of change that we advocate in this book. We aim to provide research that is accessible to working journalists, as a practical demonstration for how to enable voice through listening and, in doing so, do good journalism. We also want this project to speak to ordinary citizens who may aspire to talk and be heard, and whom much of this book is about, as a testament that they have every right to demand a news media that listens to them and takes their stories seriously.

Since the ordinary grassroots citizen is at the heart of this project, the notion of voice as the initial act of speaking and telling one's own story is our primary point of departure. The concept of voice is, however, for us and for many other theorists, inextricably linked to the act of listening. The two, voice and listening, are coupled: the accompaniment of listening, together with speaking, are two parts of the same equation where neither can be determined as entirely successful without the other (Dreher 2009).

The first and most crucial aspect is to acknowledge that everyone has a voice, and no one is voiceless. The voicelessness of the 'voiceless' is an unfortunate myth. Jan Servaes and Patchanee Malikhao (2005), for example, attest that people are 'voiceless' not because they have nothing to say, but because nobody cares to listen to them. People, all people, regardless of their personal status, class, wealth, education, gender, race or ethnicity, have something to say and have stories to tell, if only we could bear to listen. This means that simply having a voice is not enough. In addition, one needs to know that one's voice matters, that it is considered and that it is heard.

So, having a voice relies on the prerequisite of having that voice matter, to be heard and listened to by others. Active and considered listening registers and respects the distinctness and importance of the narrative of the speaker, without which voice will not succeed in being heard (Couldry 2010).

To tell one's own story is a considered decision. It requires reflection on how to speak, which part or parts of the story to tell, and what to say. Equally, listeners ought to practise critical introspection on how they listen, on what they (choose to) hear, which parts of the story they pay attention to, and which parts they ignore. This means taking an active responsibility for whom, how and what we listen to (Bickford 1996). Of course, societal and normative hierarchies often determine the trajectory of our listening, meaning that we regard some voices as more worthy of being listened to than others (more on this later). But where voice and listening are co-dependent, and if we accept that to deny the effective practice of voice to some (by not listening to them) constitutes oppression and injustice, we must also recognise that reconfiguring listening practice can potentially break up normative traditions and hierarchies, allowing greater space for a plurality of voices (Bickford 1996).

This equation of effective voice (speaking plus engaged listening) is central to the legitimacy of modern democracies. Yet, somehow, the organisation of the human sphere of communication has naturalised and made acceptable the importance of some voices over others to the extent that alternate voices do not matter (Couldry 2010). Men's voices have always mattered more than women's, so much so that this seems 'natural'. Heteronormative narratives dominate our popular culture, while homosexually aligned ones are relegated to the fringe or the obscure, and again we are duped into accepting this as 'natural', when in reality there is nothing strange or unnatural about being gay. Elite, middle-class and economically secure voices have always been mediated in abundance, relative to the voices of the poor and working classes.

Importantly, when some segments of society experience a lack of voice, when these are not listened to or heard, societal, political and cultural fissures and/or inequalities naturally arise. Denying voice to some has a material impact. Simply put, when everyone has a voice it is better for society. For example, feminism has long identified the lack of effective voice available to women as a determining factor regarding their social and economic status and inequity, as well as the related negatively connoted identity that is experienced by women in every part of the world (Macnamara 2012). The material impact of women's lack of voice is clearly evident, measureable and undeniable.

For instance, the 2019 Sustainable Development Goals Index surveyed 129 countries in terms of their progress in meeting the 2030 targets for gender equality. Not a single country in the world was found to be on track to meet these internationally agreed targets, while 2.8 billion women live in countries that are doing too little or nothing to empower women and end inequality. Women the world over still suffer diminished power and under-representation in governmental bodies, including parliaments, in upper management positions in both the private and public sector, and in the economy, while women are still unaccountably, though predominantly, paid less than men for doing the same work (Ford 2019). When half of the world's routinely marginalised voices bear direct symmetry with the same half of the world's people who are clearly afforded less social, economic and political power than the other half, the importance of effective voice as a key factor for the overall health of society becomes obvious.

And so, firstly, a considered view of voice starts with the acknowledgement that voice, *every* voice, has value. More forcefully, for societal health and in the interest of justice and equality, every voice *must* have value. It is important to not only value voice itself, but to also value the societal frameworks, institutions, platforms and resources that themselves value voice, and consciously identify, reject and reform those that do not (Couldry 2010). With regard to such societal frameworks and institutions, the media sphere is not innocent as it routinely maintains what Tanja Dreher (2009: 445) refers to as the 'hierarchies of language which can be slow to shift'. The task then 'is to take responsibility for shifting those hierarchies of attention which produce unequal opportunities for speaking and being heard. And it is "a particular kind of listening" which might serve to undo these entrenched hierarchies of voice' (Dreher 2009: 446).

Secondly, voice needs to be understood as a process, and not as a once-off isolated occurrence. Giving an account of one's life, events or conditions, telling a story or enacting the natural human activity of relating a narrative is only the first aspect of voice. Much more needs to stem from this in order for voice to be recognised, valued and effective.

For example, voice is socially grounded, meaning that it is not the isolated practice of individuals. No one narrative can be separated from an interlocking set of related narratives, which is why it is crucial to always present a particular voice in its associated context and history – something that dominant journalism often fails to do, as is evident in the following chapters (Couldry 2010).

Couldry (2010: 8) calls voice 'an embodied process' that is informed by history, and because each voice is iterated from a 'distinctive embodied position' it follows that the trajectory of each voice is distinct. Simply, we all have different things to say because we are all different. Therefore, when we fail to acknowledge and respect the inevitable differences between voices, we fail to recognise voice itself. In reality, of course, there is no *one* voice (singular), but a multiplicity of *voices* (plural). It follows then that we ought to be deeply suspicious when an institution, whose responsibility is to inform us of the events of the world, reports these from a singular (dominant) position.

Clearly, the overarching concept of voice described above involves a great many things. But, from this point on in this book, we will narrow our use of the term 'voice(s)' to a more specific connotation. That is not to exclude the importance of the concept and the process as a whole, but we do this here for simplicity and brevity. We include the bracketed '(s)' on the end of the term to invoke the possibility of the plural and to indicate a recognition that there is always more than one solitary voice related to any particular situation, story and context. For the purposes of the remainder of this book, voice(s) points to the narratives and stories of the people this book is about – the members of grassroots communities, who, all of them, have important stories to tell, whose experiences of events have implications for a broader society, country and political landscape, but whose version of events and experiences have been habitually ignored and/or misrepresented by the dominant news media.

In this book, we often refer to what we have termed the 'dominant media' for the purposes of our discussion. So what/who do we mean by the dominant media? For us, the dominant media ought to be understood less in terms of the formal structures of media ownership, but more in respect of the direction of the national narrative. That is, the myriad collection of media reports, journalists, editors, articles, broadcasts and media outlets, which collectively direct the trajectory of public discourse on any particular issue towards the same or a similar cohesive understanding of events. In overly simple terms, it is the various news media outlets and reports that all sing to the same tune, and which report on the same events in the same ways. The dominant media is then comprised of media outlets that may fall within the stable of privately owned, corporatised media conglomerates or public service media institutions, but which all behave in accordance with the dominant narrative.

We have selected the term 'dominant' to remain in keeping with Stuart Hall's (1980) outstanding and still relevant explanation of how perspectives (readings) can vary – the 'dominant' one, however, primarily orientated toward the status quo. But as much as our different perspectives and readings of events can vary, so too can our retelling of them. This book is about how there are stories, many stories, to be told about any particular scene or situation. And about how the dominant media regularly ignores most of them, in favour of telling only one story.

Importantly, the dominant media maintains the facade of professional journalism in pursuit of truth and in adherence with the highest order of media ethics. The dominant media must mythologise the profession in this way in order to ensure its own credibility. The remainder of this book, however, exposes this facade for what it is – a myth. Roland Barthes ([1957] 1972) formulates a semiotic model for the function of communicated myth, which acts as a mode of speech that is ideologically infused, but which can often operate so unobtrusively that the message is simply accepted as fact, as natural, as entirely justifiable and as the way things are. Simply, a myth is a mode of communicating an idea, the motivations of which are concealed, and the content of which is largely inaccurate, but which dupes people into believing it anyway.

In this book we have focused on three politically, socially and economically marginalised communities involved in differing struggles for social justice: these are the communities of Glebelands, Xolobeni/Amadiba and Thembelihle in South Africa. But many other marginalised groups or communities have suffered a similar non-recognition of their own voice(s) by the dominant media. We mention this here, and highlight the findings of related research studies, conducted independently of our own, to demonstrate how this media behaviour is not unique or isolated to the stories of Glebelands, Xolobeni/Amadiba and Thembelihle.

WHAT DO WE ALREADY KNOW ABOUT THE NEWS MEDIA AND VOICE(S)?

A number of other recent research studies confirm the critique that we deliver here, that the dominant media does not offer adequate voice(s) and representation to the majority of citizens, who in South

Africa predominantly are the poor. For example, a 2013 study (Malila 2013), which focused on the youth as media consumers, explored the relationships between young research participants and the media. The study highlights that young, poor, black South Africans feel mostly disconnected from the majority of news media content. Participants expressed the concern that they do not 'see' themselves in the news media, the content of which holds little relevance to their concerns, interests and lives. While South African society is bottom heavy and comprised of a large youth segment, little media content concerns the interests of the youth.

According to Jane Duncan (2013b): 'With the exception of education, youth input on issues of importance was minimal, with practically no youth input on crime. Young men were more prominent in the coverage than young women.' With close to 1000 young people surveyed in four provinces, these young people remarked on the dearth of in-depth reporting that was relevant to them. The media's failure to engage and listen to youth voice(s), and to act as an enabler for young peoples' developing civic and political identities, is striking.

In another example, in 2014, Vanessa Malila presented the findings of a news content analysis study. It revealed how the news media routinely fails to enable young persons to act as informed and engaged citizens due to neglect of representing content regarding public discourses that impact the youth. Focusing on education, the study emphasises that the news media habitually fails to provide relevant information that could be of importance to the youth in respect of education coverage. Furthermore, news reporting on education does not feature the voices, opinions or perspectives of young people – the self-same people who ought to be at the centre of the story. That young, poor, black South Africans do not recognise themselves, their interests or their communities in the dominant media, that they are not consulted, heard or listened to as a means of informing the news reporting that is directly relevant to them, is testament to the lack of engagement between the media and the majority of South Africans. The year following the publication of Malila's study saw the advent of the #FeesMustFall student-led protest movement across South Africa. While the main impetus of this movement was aimed at transforming the higher education environment, the veracity and widespread enthusiasm that characterised youth involvement in #FeesMustFall bore testament to a broad youth frustration at their lack of collective voice. Here, mass protest became the only means by which the youth were able to have their voice(s) heard or taken seriously by the establishment.

Let us shift focus for a minute, from the youth to another under-represented, marginalised and stereotyped segment of society, and one that comprises just over half of all people alive in the world: women. A 2013 report conducted by the media monitoring company, Media Tenor, found that women's voices are routinely under-represented in the news media, and on television women accounted for only 14 per cent of coverage in South Africa (Duncan 2013b). This problem is not only endemic to South Africa, but in most regions of the world.

In 2014 the United Nations Educational, Scientific and Cultural Organization (UNESCO) released its report, 'World Trends in Freedom of Expression and Media Development', which highlighted the global extent of the matter. Women constitute less than a quarter (24 per cent) of the persons heard or represented in traditional news media, but, even worse, women comprise only a fifth of authoritative news voices quoted in the news (20 per cent of experts and 19 per cent as spokespersons). News outlets looking for expert comment or interviewees on matters of societal, legal, political or economic importance will consult a man about 81 per cent of the time (UNESCO 2014). Women working in the media sector, who are best placed to increase the gendered diversity of news media reporting, are often shifted to 'soft news' beats, relegated to covering topics traditionally considered to be more feminine, such as celebrity gossip or fashion news, while their male colleagues report on the important stuff, such as politics and the economy.

In 2018, I was asked to assist with the editorial work on the more recent 2018 edition of the UNESCO World Trends report. While studying the findings compiled for each of the six world regions, I discovered how the position of women in the media sector and their levels of representation had not only stagnated rather than improved since 2014, but in some regions and contexts had actually regressed (UNESCO 2018).

I was later asked to attend the UNESCO World Press Freedom Day Conference held in Accra, Ghana, and speak to the contents of the 2018 report. While the UNESCO report covers a range of topics, including media freedom, independence, diversity and the safety of journalists around the world, it was the stagnation and in some places the regression of women's positions in the media that most startled me. Here we are, talking about approximately 52 per cent of all peoples, in the twenty-first century, and after decades-long myriad efforts by global, multilateral and non-governmental organisations to curb the under-representation of women in the news, as well as support the promotion of women media workers, but all the while very little appears to have changed. Women journalists are still predominantly paid less than men. Only one in four media decision-makers are women, one in five experts interviewed are women, and one in three reporters are women – and these will likely not be assigned to 'hard news' coverage (UNESCO 2018). On this, I said:

> Women's potential for the advancement of media diversity and pluralism is more nuanced and multi-layered than simply promoting more women to senior management level within media organisations. The broader representation of women, by women, stands to not only increase media profits (by behaving more inclusively toward more of the audience) but improve the overall health of the media ecology and markets. Women do not write about the world in the same way as men, but that does not mean that the only things that they have something to say about are lifestyle issues like fashion or celebrity gossip. Women think, feel, know, give-a-damn, and write, about things like politics, corruption, war, and the law just as well as men do – albeit and thankfully, quite differently from them (Reid 2018b).

Some of the members of the audience smiled. Most of the audience, and especially the women present, clapped. The collection of men in the audience, who visibly frowned, grunted with disapproval and/or shook their heads, did not escape my notice.

It would be easy to assume that these global figures are skewed mostly by the inclusion of numbers from media systems that operate in countries that are undemocratic or authoritarian regimes. But, the statistics for women's inclusion in the media is only a few percentage points higher in most so-called democratic countries. A stark reminder that we still have a long way to go in encouraging the naturalisation and societal acceptance of a broader representation of women's voice(s) in the dominant media surfaced recently in the United Kingdom. On 3 September 2018, the BBC broadcast the first episode of its new lunchtime political discussion programme, *Politics Live*. The show is anchored by a woman, Jo Coburn. The panel was comprised of two members of parliament, the BBC's political editor, *The Guardian*'s joint political editor and a journalist from the *Daily Telegraph*. That is an admirable collection of persons for a panel, the purpose of which is to discuss politics. As luck would have it, all of the invited panellists for that day also happened to be women.

The social media backlash from men was immediate. Male social media users accused the panel of being a stunt, saying that the show was gimmicky, too politically correct and compared it to a UK daytime celebrity news and lifestyle talk show called *Loose Women*. The *Politics Live* editor, Rob Burley, publically defended the fact that the panel featured five women in a manner he would have undoubtedly not had to do if it had featured five men (Lyons 2018). Still, even today, dominant societal discourses are so deeply imbued with the patriarchal naturalisation of male voice that a mere instance of the representation of women's voice(s) is considered offensive.

Another often misrepresented collection of voice(s) is public protestors. A study conducted by academics at the University of Cape Town (Wasserman, Bosch and Chuma 2018) examined the media's coverage of community protest action in South Africa, and explored the views of the activists involved in arranging the protests.

Tellingly, the 2018 study found that while journalists 'approached the protests from the conventional "news values" perspective which they considered natural, activists felt that the mainstream media somehow short-changed them and their causes by either misrepresenting them or highlighting the voices of authorities and other "official" sources while at the same time marginalising ordinary citizens' voices' (Wasserman, Bosch and Chuma 2018: 379).

> In the case of South African activists, the overwhelming sentiment was that while the media played an important role in covering the protests and keeping them on the public agenda, the manner of coverage was 'top-down' in that it privileged elite voices and frames of reference while marginalising the ordinary citizens on the ground. While some activists viewed the media as an essential part of modern politics, others said that the media did not speak to the audiences they were trying to reach, so in these instances, it was considered marginal (Wasserman, Bosch and Chuma 2018: 380).

Perhaps the most iconic example of the dominant media's misrepresentation of the stories of the poor in post-1994 South Africa surfaced with the reportage of the Marikana massacre. On 12 August 2012, a large group of miners, who had been striking for a period of six days, gathered together to protest their low wages on an open patch of arid land close to the Lonmin mine near the town of Rustenburg. After a tense stand-off between the miners and the police, the miners began to disperse. At that moment, the South African Police Service (SAPS) opened fire on the dispersing protestors, shooting 112 of them, wounding 78 and killing 34. What made the massacre more appalling was that this was not a simple case of spontaneous panic on the part of the police officers present. Initial news media reports gave a shocked South African public the impression that the police had opened fire in panic, perhaps because they believed that their own lives were in danger from a group of slowly approaching miners, and, by the time a ceasefire had been called and obeyed, 112 protestors had unfortunately been shot. The official SAPS version of events maintained that the police officers on the scene acted in self-defence.

But this is not what really happened. What really happened is much more horrifying. The first volley of gunfire, and the only shooting incident initially reported in the news, downed only a small group of miners. The remainder of the 112 people shot were thereafter quite literally hunted down by SAPS officers as they tried to run away, many of them shot in the back. This second and brutal round of killings was not reported by the press.

It was an academic, It was an academic (not a journalist), Peter Alexander, who first alerted us to the full extent, nature and character of the police killings on that day. He and his team of researchers worked the scene, recorded evidence and collected eyewitness accounts (Alexander et al. 2012). Finally, almost a month after the massacre, an independent journalist, Greg Marinovich (2012), writing for the independent publication *Daily Maverick*, reported on the second killing sites where many people had been shot while trying to hide from the police, were trapped, and shot at close range. Until this point, the dominant news media, without exception and like well-behaved sheep, had dutifully reported the account provided by government and police spokespersons, which painted the massacre as an unfortunate accident. Marinovich's article cracked that facade wide open.

The Marikana massacre subsequently initiated a period of scrutiny aimed at the news media's poor performance (Reid 2012). Duncan (2012) performed a content analysis of 153 articles published in mainstream newspapers (*Business Day, The Star, New Age, The Citizen, The Times, Sowetan, Beeld, Die Burger* and *Mail & Guardian*) between 13 and 22 August 2012. In particular, Duncan analysed the sources consulted by journalists in the run-up to and the immediate aftermath of the massacre. She revealed that miners were used as sources for information in only 3 per cent of the news articles sampled. This is astonishing, since it was only the miners themselves who could provide first-hand eyewitness accounts to the police actions. Nonetheless, the majority of sources of information consulted by news outlets were business (27 per cent), mine management/owners (14 per cent), political parties (10 per cent), government (9 per cent) and the SAPS (5 per cent).

Duncan (2012) says:

> Of the 3 percent of miners who were interviewed … only one worker was quoted speaking about what actually happened during the massacre, and he said the police shot first. Most miners were interviewed in relation to the stories alleging that the miners had used muti [traditional medicine] to defend themselves against the police's bullets, as well as the miners' working and living conditions. So in other words, of all 153 articles, only one showed any attempt by a journalist to obtain an account from a worker about their version of events. There is scant evidence of journalists having asked the miners the simplest and most basic of questions, namely 'what happened'?

The findings of Duncan's (2012) study highlight two central aspects in respect of the news media's iteration of voice(s). Firstly, where the people who are most directly impacted by events are not consulted, crucial information is often missed, thus devaluing the accuracy of journalistic reporting. Rule number one: talk to the people who were actually there, even if they are poor. Secondly, and central to the practice of meaningful listening encompassing a respect for the dignity of voice(s), journalists not only need to interview the people concerned, but also actually listen to them. For journalists, talking to people on the ground should not amount to a mere tick-the-box exercise. Had journalists really listened to the scant few miners they did interview in the wake of the Marikana massacre, they would have heard detailed narratives that would have provided them with more information about events than simply the types of *muti* used as protection from bullets.

Of course, this lack of listening is not a characteristic that is unique to the South African dominant media, but occurs all over the world. On this, Penny O'Donnell (2009: 505) states the following: 'There is no doubt that Journalism 1.0 has a poor track record in reporting experiences of social marginalisation; the social groups most commonly absent or spoken for by the media include poor women, Indigenous people, migrants who do not speak the official common language, and young people.'

MOTIVATION FOR THIS BOOK

So, why did we write this book? As mentioned, many recent research projects provide evidence of the news media's habitual misrepresentation or non-representation of the voice(s) belonging to the largest segment of the country's population, the marginalised and poor. Conversely, the news media is disproportionately dominated by narratives that serve the interests of, speak to and speak about the small segments of the population that retain political, social and economic power (see, for example, Berger 2003; Duncan 2012; Friedman 2011; Garman and Malila 2017; Malila 2013, 2014; Malila and Garman 2016; Reid 2012; Wasserman 2013, 2017; Wasserman, Chuma and Bosch 2016).

The amount of literature providing evidence-based research that presents the earlier or similar findings is steadily growing. The dominant news media does a poor job of reporting grassroots and ordinary citizens' voice(s), and researchers have proved it. However, the majority of research projects that tackle this problem do not do two important but crucial things. The first of these is that the researchers who critique the news media's lack of engagement with voice(s) do not do precisely what they insist journalists ought to do. That is, researchers most often do not engage with the very people for whom they claim to speak. The largest body of research literature here relies on various types of media content analysis as a measure to demonstrate the lack of adequately represented voice(s) in news reportage. However, apart from a select few exceptions, most researchers do not themselves engage with or listen to the persons whom they claim the media misrepresents. Recent exceptions to this include Duncan (2016), Malila (2017) and Wasserman, Bosch and Chuma (2018).

Secondly, most of the literature on the news media's behaviour towards voice(s) provides critique only but does not attempt to provide alternative ways of doing things, nor suggest practical ways in which to change the way we make news. Critique is important. But it is also important to follow through with explorations of how things can be done differently, to change things for the better.

This book attempts to fill both of the gaps highlighted above. First, we set out to actively participate in a thorough process of listening, with a deep respect for the dignity of voice(s). We did this because we do not believe that we can encourage journalists to do so if we are not committed to doing so ourselves. We also did this as a means of demonstration. Quite simply, we wanted to show that it can be done. Secondly, we did not write this book only to complain about the news media's behaviour, but also to offer suggested recommendations for how to encourage a more participative practice of listening among journalists, in the interest of democratising the media sphere. Only once we understand the machinations of dominant media behaviour and how these negatively impact the inclusion of voice(s), can we begin to explore alternative methods to traditional, dominant news production.

METHODOLOGY AND SUMMARY OF CHAPTERS

The methodology for this book involved various avenues, focusing primarily on a set of in-depth interviews, a large-scale media content analysis and a survey of relevant related research. The book presents three case studies/stories, which capture a representational cross-section of struggle narratives from poor communities in both rural and urban post-1994 South Africa. Each of these case studies encompasses differing but crucial historical, geographical and socio-political 'characteristics' of the post-1994 period.

Those characteristics include, but are not wholly limited to, issues of:

- land – its ownership/distribution, usage and associated relations of production;
- basic services (such as water, electricity, education, health care, housing) – availability, affordability and provision;
- social and productive relationships with/involving the state and the private sector, inclusive of corruption and undemocratic practice;
- the levels, content and history of political and social activism – both in respect of organisations and collectives established in communities and active in various struggles and vis-à-vis the dominant broader political trends and party politics; and
- geographical location and ethnographic make-up.

Underlying all of these is the larger issue of the ways in which the developmental experiences of each specific community and the struggles in which it has engaged have been shaped by the dominant (macro) post-1994 political economy of South Africa, inclusive of the news media terrain.

Glebelands is the largest hostel community in South Africa, situated in Umlazi, South Durban. Over the last decade, in particular, Glebelands has experienced intense and violent struggles (including over 160 murders or assassinations since April 2014) centred on political and ethnic mobilisation, control of accommodation, and police and political party/state complicity in violence and corruption.

The Amadiba region encompasses several rural villages along the Wild Coast region of the Eastern Cape Province. The Amadiba community has been involved in lengthy struggles centred on the issuing of mining rights on their land as well as associated road construction. These have involved all levels of the state as well as private mining corporations. The Amadiba Crisis Committee (ACC), a community-based organisation, has for many years been at the forefront of opposing the proposed dune mining in the Xolobeni area. In March 2016, the chairperson of the ACC, Sikhosiphi 'Bazooka' Radebe, was assassinated.

Thembelihle is an urban, semi-informal community situated in the Johannesburg Metro, near Soweto. Thembelihle has a long history of social justice struggle centred on housing, forced relocation, urban development, political party contestation and the right to protest. Members of this community have routinely been subjected to acute police brutality, and have been arrested and wrongfully detained, while community leaders and organisers have been personally targeted by security services, having their homes raided by the police, their families and children intimidated and some have been forced into hiding.

In doing the research for this book, we engaged with relevant organisations and activists who both work with and live in each of the communities. This was followed by setting up a range of in-depth interviews in each community. We made physical visits to the communities to conduct the interviews and in order to get the real, full, detailed and bottom-up versions of the respective stories.

A full-scale media content analysis was conducted in order to determine how the stories relevant to each of these three communities were represented by the dominant media, as well as how these stories have been communicated by the relevant centres of power, including government. Through collating a range of research materials, as well as interview transcripts, and then through critical analysis, the book places these all within the macro socio-economic and political context of South Africa since 1994. This then allows a demonstration of how the accumulated evidence exposes the gap between the actual/real stories of these communities and those told by the dominant media, and, in the process, exposes the mistruths, myths and self-interested motivation behind the dominant discourse and thought frame that characterises the storytelling of the dominant news media.

We followed a similar methodology of combining a media content analysis coupled with in-depth interviews to Duncan's 2016 study, when she investigated the news media's reportage of protests and protestors in the regions of Rustenburg, Mbombela, Blue Crane Route (focusing specifically on Cookhouse) and the Nelson Mandela Bay Metro. 'These were the sites where in-depth interviews were conducted … so the narratives of the protestors could be compared and contrasted with the main narratives in the news articles' (Duncan 2016: 150). While Duncan was dealing specifically with the representation of protest and protestors, and we set out to investigate the stories not necessarily of protestors, but of particular communities involved in struggles with high news value, the methodology adopted by Duncan nonetheless proved instructive. Perhaps not surprisingly, however, the character of Duncan's (2016) findings was similar to ours regarding the manner in which the dominant media routinely applied negative and stereotypical frames to the stories of the poor, as opposed to the markedly different stories told by the people themselves.

In short, this book aims to provide a long-overdue opportunity for these groups of marginalised and downtrodden peoples to practise voice, to tell their stories as they have lived and experienced them during the post-apartheid period, and for those stories to be inserted into the overall public sphere of national debate.

Chapter 2 describes the manner in which we approached the interview process. Knowing that we wished to surface a multiplicity of voice(s) from the three communities of Glebelands, Xolobeni and Thembelihle, we initially needed to rethink and interrogate our own strategies of listening. This chapter also contextualises the social and economic landscape of post-1994 South Africa, and presents the architecture of how we constructed the retelling of the collected narratives of the three communities.

Chapters 3, 4 and 5 form the heart of the book. Here, the stories of the three selected communities are first briefly contextualised within the larger developmental and political economy of contemporary South Africa. This allowed us to better appreciate both the political and socioeconomic location and the importance of these stories. The remainder of each chapter focuses on surfacing voices from each of the three communities. Each community sub-section begins with a concise history/biography of the community, followed by excerpts taken from the interviews conducted, which are organised according to various topics that are relevant to the community context and associated stories.

In chapter 6, the focus is turned towards the dominant media, whose character and content (when it comes to covering the marginalised and the poor) is revealed as being in core service to a profit-driven model and elitist narrative. To empirically back up this argument, the chapter proceeds to provide a succinct cross-section analysis covering all three communities, including examples selected from a comprehensive post-1994 sampling of print articles and audio-visual clips from numerous media outlets that constitute the dominant media in South Africa. In doing so, the analysis serves two reinforcing purposes: to reveal key differences, contradictions, omissions and indeed completely opposite 'tellings' between the stories told by the residents and those contained in the dominant media; and to subject the storytelling of the dominant media to both objective and subjective critique.

Chapter 7 provides a framing of South Africa's post-1994 macro socio-economic and political realities of unequal relations of class, racial and gender position and power, which produce societal dominance in various ways. It is within this macro framing that the presence, content and character, as well as practical role, of South Africa's dominant media can be properly conceptualised and understood. This is done by offering a double-sided analysis-argument of the dialectic of this dominance, backed up by the use of selected parts of the stories told by community members, as well as examples taken from media articles. On the one hand, it shows the ways in which dominant narratives have rooted and shaped the developmental experiences and life possibilities of the targeted communities and their struggles. On the other hand, it reveals the ways in which the dominant media has foundationally constructed a dominant thought frame and discourse that has enabled, reflected and moulded a dominant way of seeing and thinking about poor communities and their struggles and thus also of how their related stories are told.

We then turn our attention in chapters 8, 9 and 10 to how this media behaviour can and ought to be changed, as well as the benefits of doing so. Chapter 8 addresses the double-edged predicament faced by much of the world's dominant news media presently, that is, the crisis of credibility and a crisis of financial sustainability. The chapter investigates how these could both be alleviated through increased levels of media content diversity, with an emphasis on the inclusion of marginalised voice(s).

In chapter 9, we discuss how critical debates on news media behaviour have regularly been scuppered by illogical arguments that equate legitimate critique with intolerable 'attacks' on the freedom of the press. This mythologisation of the journalistic profession, which places it beyond reproach and is framed in catchphrases like 'journalism is not a crime', often act as a hindrance to constructive debates on how the news media could perform better. Indeed, critique is also not a crime. The chapter argues for a redefinition of the popular understanding of media freedom to one that includes a concern for audience-centred freedoms, and, by implication, a re-evaluation of related concepts within the spectrum of journalistic ethics, as well as a revamp of media accountability mechanisms.

Chapter 10 makes case for 'listening journalism', which is an already well-established concept in media and communications theory, but which has been largely ignored in practice, both by media critics, academics and researchers and by the news media industry. The in-depth investigation and reportage on each of the three selected communities presented in this book serves as an example of listening journalism/research in practice, as it could be applied more broadly by the press, and as an example of how to retell stories from the ground in a way that does not further marginalise poor communities but gives them a legitimate voice in the public sphere. Lastly, the chapter addresses the need to encourage a realignment of the paradigms governing the journalistic profession, the manner in which journalists are taught and trained within the higher education environment, and offers a set of practical guidelines for working journalists wishing to engage in meaningful listening journalism.

THE AUDIENCE-CENTRED APPROACH

The research performed for this book was commissioned by the Media Policy and Democracy Project (MPDP) and funded by the Open Society

Foundation for South Africa and the Women in Research grant provided by the University of South Africa (UNISA). The MPDP was launched in 2012 and is a South African-based research collective, administrated jointly between the Department of Communication Science at UNISA and the Department of Journalism, Film and Television at the University of Johannesburg. It aims to promote participatory media and communications policymaking in the public interest.

Since its launch, the MPDP has collaborated with academics and researchers from various institutions throughout South Africa and the world. The MPDP has also collaborated with civil society organisations and social justice movements, which have a specific focus on media and communications policymaking, and which have a central concern for the public interest and a ground-up audience-based approach to research and policy interventions. Part of the work of the MPDP includes consultation with national media policymakers, including parliament, in order to inject media policymaking processes with informed, evidence-based research that holds a concern for the public interest at its core. The combined and collective efforts of MPDP researchers has contributed to policymaking involving media and internet freedom, public service broadcasting and digital terrestrial television, journalistic ethics and accountability systems, including press regulation, mass communications surveillance and privacy, as well as media diversity and transformation.

Central to this research collective is an untraditional mode of performing research developed by the MPDP, the audience-centred approach. In a manner that is dissimilar to Northern-developed research practices, the audience-centred approach regards the audience, the media end user, the ordinary person on the ground as primary and central to the research effort (Duncan and Reid 2013; Reid 2017a, 2018a). Each of our research efforts begins by taking the perspective of the audience/grassroots citizen as its point of departure. The audience-centred approach is not a research methodology; it is a research attitude. Our methodologies are multiple and vary because in each case they will depend entirely on the direction received from a particular ground-up departure point and the specificities of each contextual situation relative to the relationship this bears with the media or communications land-scape.

For the most part, the trajectory of media policymaking is directed by those with the power and means to do so, whether they are media owners and stakeholders, corporate capital, elites in government or political circles or media regulators. As a ground-up approach to research and media policymaking, the audience-centred approach inverts the traditional top-down power axis, and operates according to the understanding that the media audience is the primary point of departure and ought to direct the progression of policymaking and research.

Clearly, the audience-centred approach can be comfortably situated within the broader context and discourse of decolonial approaches to scholarship, particularly within media studies. Our primary aim in this book is not to offer new theoretical contributions to the decolonial debate on scholarship and research, but rather to present a practical example of what such approaches may look like in practice. While the transformative trajectory of decolonial discourse on teaching, learning, training and research holds immeasurable value, much of this debate remains on a theoretical, general and somewhat abstract level. We attest that actively listening to what grassroots communities have to say, and taking their stories seriously, is one way in which to move beyond traditional Western epistemologies.

We adopt the audience-centred approach because firstly and as social scientists, we have a moral obligation to do so; and secondly, because the audience-centred approach centres its efforts on a respect for the dignity of voice(s); and thirdly, because it just makes sense: if we want to research the media, then surely the best place to start is with the peoples whom the media ought to exist for. And if not for the audience/media end users, then what or who is the media for? Further, and more acutely, without the audience/media end users, would the media even have a purpose? Simply, the media exits because of the audience. How then can we operate if the audience and its voice(s) are anything but central?

PART 1

FROM THE INSIDE: VOICE(S) FROM THE GROUND

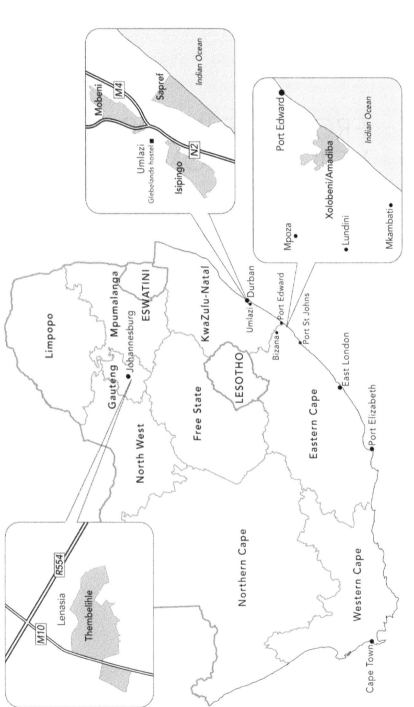

Figure 2.1: Map of South Africa showing the three communities that provide the case studies: Xolobeni/Amadiba, Glebelands, and Thembelihle

2

Community Perspective, Experience and Voice

Julie Reid and Dale T. McKinley

Asmall number of mostly independent news outlets acknowledge that the real 'experts' on any particular news story are the people whose lives are most impacted by the events and situations that the stories describe. The *Global Press Journal* employs reporters who are based within the community about which they report, recognising the value of journalism that is informed by an understanding of local languages, local customs and contexts, and local histories, so that information is framed in a culturally and contextually appropriate way.

Managing editor of the *Global Press Journal*, Krista Kapralos (2018) describes what she terms the 'reliability gap': a phenomenon in dominant news journalism where predominantly Western media groups and news outlets collect and represent data and evidence based on Western normative standards, regardless of whether the situation being reported on is geographically or culturally Western. Kapralos (2018) adds:

When one culture sets the standard for truth (and implements that standard regardless of location), the narratives that culture culls from other places are likely to be warped ... For many research and news agencies, the process of gathering data results in a continual confrontation between Western assumptions and non-Western cultures. While that reality makes the truth less convenient to find, there is a huge potential payoff for those who seek it in context: A meaningful negotiation between equal partners who can respectfully create systems to help determine what is true. At *Global Press Journal*, we believe it's difficult – if not impossible – to determine the truth without engaging local people. Every story we publish is reported by a local person. Every story includes sources who are as close as possible to the situations described. And reporters are supported by a robust editorial team dedicated to accuracy.

The Guardian's editor-in-chief, Katharine Viner, insists that media outlets ought to be much more representative of the societies they aim to represent. A survey conducted in the United Kingdom revealed that a privately educated elite still dominates that country's journalism profession, and that journalism has revealed a trend towards social exclusivity more than any other profession (Weale 2016; Jones 2016). According to Viner (2017), 'This matters because people from exclusive, homogenous backgrounds are unlikely to know anyone adversely affected by the crises of our era, or to spend time in the places where they are happening. Media organisations staffed largely by people from narrow backgrounds are less likely to recognise the issues that people notice in their communities every day as "news"; the discussions inside such organisations will inevitably be shaped by the shared privilege of the participants.' Similar to the UK, South Africa's public sphere is still very much an elite sphere, and mediated national conversations on matters of public interest are predominantly determined by the interests of this elite (Duncan 2013b; Friedman 2011).

There is a societal danger in the routine exclusion of some voices while over-amplifying others. A society risks only becoming aware of a mounting crisis at the grassroots level when it is too late and when there is a social explosion, such as the critical events and subsequent massacre at Marikana (Duncan 2013b). But even when not taking such extreme dangers into account, the problem of the inequitable representation of voice still matters. The most basic and fundamental societal mandate of the news media is to inform: to provide audiences with accurate, trustworthy and relevant information about the world around them.

Regarding the South African news media, this means representing a realistic picture of the country. But this is a country that includes, and is predominantly populated by, the economically marginalised and poor. Yet, voice(s) from this societal sector are habitually excluded. The segment of society that enjoys the largest representation of mediated voice is but a small portion of the citizenry. How then, are we to know what is going on in our world when we are presented with such a limited picture? Additionally, when so under-informed about a broader spectrum of realities, how can we realistically initiate national discourses aimed at societal coherence, economic development or the meaningful promotion of social justice? In simple terms, how can we solve our own problems when we have very little idea of what is really going on?

PUTTING VOICE(S) FIRST

The various research studies mentioned in chapter 1 examined the (mis)representation of voice(s) particular to a specific marginalised profile or demographic, that is, the youth, women or protestors. In this book we chose to follow a slightly different approach, and, instead of examining a broad category of marginalised persons, honed in instead on three very particular communities and sites where stories of high news value have played out. The demographic of the people we spoke to was then of secondary importance to us.

Of primary importance were the stories that each individual had to tell – their personal iteration of voice, which, of course, was nonetheless imbued with their particular demographic identity. By collecting the stories and first-hand accounts of persons who had actually lived through a particular set of events, we were able to then compare the contents of these first-hand accounts to the way in which these same events had been retold by the dominant news media. It is only a small adjustment of methodological focus, but it makes all the difference. A detailed comparison to news media content is not possible when examining the perspectives of a particular demographic of participant regardless of their individual position: here, even though each participant may belong to a similar demographic, each will have experienced a different set of events. Instead, we opted to talk to people who had lived through a particular set of events by focusing on the geographic communities where those events had taken place, meaning that we could thereafter compare the collected first-hand accounts to the manner in which these events had been retold by the dominant media.

Another important shift in methodological focus was that when we interviewed our participants, we did not approach the interview with a stringent, predetermined set of must-ask questions. Given the centrality of voice(s) to this project, we knew that we had to interrogate our own strategies of listening. On a purely practical level, this meant we needed to rethink how we were going to approach the interviews with the different participants from the three communities that we were working with in order to best allow them adequate space to narrate their own stories.

We did not ask the people we talked with to focus on any particular aspect, event or key category as identified by us. We only asked them to do one thing: we asked them to tell their story. We found that in allowing them to claim as much lateral narrative space as they liked, they related to us in far more depth, detail and richness of content than if we had interjected and tried to force their responses to focus on any set of stringent predetermined categories or questions.

Of course, this is not always a comfortable thing for a researcher or a journalist to do. We are trained to get straight to the core of a story in the least time possible, to focus only on the 'facts' and ignore unnecessary waffle. The arrogance of this approach, however, is that it too often denies the respectful iteration of voice(s). Firstly, it assumes a position of power on the part of the researcher or journalist. It is the researcher and/or journalist who will decide what information is relevant and what is not and will guide the engagement accordingly. The arrogance of the myth of the 'expert' here disenables the notion of voice as a process of engagement and all of the richness that lies therein.

Social scientists and journalists, however, are problematically trained to approach interviews with a predetermined set of criteria in mind, or a set of research goals and objectives, which then determines the trajectory of the inflexibly formulated interview guideline or schedule (a preset list of questions that have to be asked of each interviewee). Researchers will tell you that this has to be done to ensure consistency, reliability and validity in the data, as if people's personal accounts of their experiences and lives can be properly described by a term as impersonal as 'data'. Journalists will tell you that this approach is necessary in order to collect only those 'facts' that are of relevance to the news story they are piecing together, as if the only parts of peoples' stories that are relevant are the ones that we in our supposed 'expert' knowledge deem to be relevant. But as journalists and researchers, who are we, really, to say what is relevant and what is not with regard to an event that we have not lived, are not personally impacted by and of which we have no situational or historical experience? Who, then, is the real 'expert' on the story if not the people whose lives are directly determined by it?

Secondly, when we are too hasty to arrive at only the 'facts' of an isolated event, we too often miss, overlook and disregard important contextual and historical details that would more accurately inform understandings of current events. Again, this approach ignores voice as an embodied process, that it is socially grounded and that each narrative retelling of events is only one part of a broader interlocking set of related narratives.

Thirdly, the narrow, delimiting and sound-bite-driven approach to interviewing so often applied by researchers and journalists ignorantly and arrogantly bears little respect for difference and diversity, which is another key aspect in the value of voice. Again, where each voice is distinct, the failure to recognise the differences between voices is a failure to recognise voice at all. However, an engagement with the multiplicity of voice(s) that are able to speak to one event requires more patience than what the narrow, more traditional approach to interviewing allows.

Fourthly, a narrow and limited approach to interviewing does not do much in terms of respecting human dignity, or in terms of treating people as if they do in fact know how to tell their own stories. Further, simply claiming (or being allowed) the room to narrate one's own story, or speaking, is not sufficient to effect the successful process of voice. To afford dignity to the speaker, then the speaker must know that their voice matters and that it is heard (Couldry 2010: 1). But do these voice(s) really matter to us if we insist that they only speak to the particular predetermined categories that we have established before the engagement even commences?

THE CURRENT CONTEXT: POST-1994 SOUTH AFRICA

> Every age has its own fascism, and we see the warning signs wherever the concentration of power denies citizens the possibility and the means of expressing and acting on their own free will. There are many ways of reaching this point ... by denying and distorting information ... and by spreading in a myriad subtle ways nostalgia for a world where order reigned, and where the security of a privileged few depends on the forced labour and the forced silence of the many.
> — Levi in Pugliese 2016

While South Africa is certainly not a fascist state, there are just as certainly enough warning signs that should arouse serious concern for all of those who have sacrificed and continue to struggle for a vibrant and healthy democracy. As Primo Levi notes in the epigraph above, it is particularly when concentrated power and the interests of the elite begin to consistently undermine the realm of free expression, will and information – all of which are indispensable to democratic action and voice – that we should be more than concerned.

Such undermining has been well entrenched within South Africa's political, economic and social fabric for generations, including, even if differentially applied and experienced, in the post-1994 democratic era. This is nowhere more so than when it comes to the dominant media and the perspectives, experiences and voices of poor communities. Much like the country's economy, the media sector is highly monopolised and, as such, exclusivist in its DNA. More specifically, at the core foundation of this exclusivity is class, buttressed by considerations of race, gender and sexuality.

Here is the class reality: South Africa has 'world-class' inequality where 75 per cent of the aggregate wealth is held by the top 10 per cent of the population, while the bottom 50 per cent hold a mere 2.5 per cent (Simkins 2014). Not surprisingly, the overall number of people living in poverty – measured as an 'upper bound poverty line' of R779 (in 2016 rand) per month, per person – stands at 54 per cent (StatsSA 2015).

In structural terms then, the dominant media largely speak for and to the dominant class. In practical terms, this translates into the perspectives, experiences and voices of the majority of people who live and work in South Africa, and who are poor, being treated as peripheral. There are few better examples of this than Jane Duncan's exposé of the coverage of the Marikana massacre by the dominant media, which clearly reveals the consequent structural and practical class bias, as described in chapter 1 (Duncan 2013a). If only one side of the story is told or is so dominant as to effectively sideline and/or caricature any counter-narrative or competing story, then the conceptual frame and practical approach of the individual reader and societal consumer can only serve to reinforce ignorance, division and untruths.

That is why it is so crucial, not simply in respect of exposing and contesting the 'storytelling' of the dominant media but to defending and sustaining democracy itself, that the stories of the poor majority are listened to and communicated.

Herein lies the basis for the research that underpins this book. The three communities that provide the case studies – Glebelands, Xolobeni/Amadiba and Thembelihle – were chosen because they capture a representational cross section of struggle stories from poor communities in both rural and urban post-1994 South Africa. In other words, each of these case studies encompasses ('represents') differing but crucial historical, geographical and socio-political characteristics of the post-1994 period within a larger tableau of ongoing socio-political contestation and class (read: economic) conflict.

Taken together, these stories can therefore provide a critical counter-narrative to that of the dominant media (and oftentimes to that of government as well). They can also assist with revealing the ways in which the developmental experiences of the specific community, and the struggles in which it has engaged, have been shaped by the (macro) post-1994 political economy of South Africa, inclusive of the dominant media terrain. And further, they can go some way to help explain and understand the exigencies of power and inequality that have characterised South Africa's broader democratic journey.

STORIES FROM THREE COMMUNITIES

In the following three chapters, we present stories from the communities of Glebelands, Xolobeni/Amadiba and Thembelihle as they were related to us by the people who live there. From the very beginning, we had to acknowledge our own role in 'remaking' these stories as they would eventually appear here in this book, where we have essentially acted as intermediaries for making meaning. This role of acting as an intermediary is one that is shared by social science researchers and journalists alike when we behave as the conduits for carrying meaning and messages from the ground to published content. The nuance, however, comes in how this work of intermediation is performed. What choices does the intermediate make, and what principle of intermediation is followed?

On a purely practical level, we knew we had to find a way to 'retell' the many narratives related to us in a manner that would give prominence to these voice(s) themselves, while also working as a coherent and easy-to-follow reportage of an incredibly complex set of interrelated narratives. As much as it is important to allow lateral space for people to practise voice and to relate their own stories, it is equally crucial for such voice(s) to be 'packaged' in such a way as to be easily understandable to the reader. The role of the intermediary here is tricky and imbued with heavy responsibility: 'tricky' because narrative material must be translated in its form (though not its content) to function as an easily accessible text, while remaining cognisant of a responsibility to the people whose voices are informing that text, and to retell their stories with respect, dignity and truth.

For us, it would have made little sense to simply provide hundreds of pages of interview transcripts from 22 different interviews across three separate communities, quoted here verbatim. While this would have been the most accurate reflection of all things that were said, it would not have accomplished a satisfactory retelling of voice(s) in terms of readability. Instead, we decided to arrange the different aspects of the narratives given to us thematically, extract corresponding parts of the interviews and then organise and integrate excerpts into the larger body of text that seeks to 'tell' the respective stories and enable the inclusion of associated voice(s). To fulfil this task, the stories of each community are 'told' by breaking them down into eight distinct focal areas or topics.

The eight focal areas we selected for use are particular to this project. They were selected for their relevance to the specific social, political and environmental contexts of the three communities. Suffice to say that other researchers and/or journalists following a similar model of listening may develop alternative or additional focal areas or topics specific to the contexts of the communities or peoples with whose voice(s) they engage. But we believe that the fundamental principles of this approach would remain the same, that is, that every voice has a value, that each voice is distinct, that voice is an ongoing process and that voice is socially grounded, being situated within a particular historical context. Below, each of the focal areas that we selected to employ is set out with a brief explanation and motivation.

One: The personal side

Rarely do the dominant media offer much more than, at best, a cursory glance at the personal lives and experiences of activists and residents in poor communities. Including these is essential because it humanises the individual, the associated events or struggles as well as the community itself and creates a bridge between the reader and the community/ residents to better locate and understand the subject matter and those involved.

Two: History and context of the area

It is crucially important to cover the overall frame of conditions of life, socio-political conflict as well as the organisations and/or individuals involved (whether internal or external). Without this, one's view and understanding will have no historical background, no contextual foundation and no means of assessing and/or determining facts, interpretations and explanations of the hows and whys of what has happened. If we recognise voice as a socially grounded process, then voice(s) can only be properly understood by placing it within the associated history and context.

Three: Community organisation

While this varies widely according to the community, it is vital to provide a clear sense of the reasons behind the formation of the organisation or collective, its relationships (internal and external), core purpose and overall trajectory, as well as the main experiences in struggle. Doing so also allows for the surfacing of any divisions within the community and how this plays out and is understood.

Four: Role of the state

This applies both proactively and reactively and allows for particular attention to be given to the state's approach to and activity around community protest and voice, as well as official or legal spaces, combined with avenues and institutions for community participation and redress. Where applicable, this also provides an opportunity to include the role and activities of traditional authorities.

Five: Role of political parties

Political parties are most often at the heart of community politics and conflict, more particularly through local councillors, as well as through influence over key local state and governance structures and institutions. As such, their role and activity is central to shaping the character and content of community life and struggle.

Six: Role of law enforcement and the courts

Given the conflictual nature of community stories being 'told', it is important to surface the continuities and contradictions of related actions or reactions, complaints for redress, justice and accountability, as well as any measures taken to address these, both immediately and over time.

Seven: The dominant and other media

Rarely are the opinions and experiences that poor people have of the dominant media ever surfaced with any kind of depth and detail. Not only does this allow for a more grounded appraisal and critique but, it also provides space for surfacing the specifics of how the dominant media's coverage and portrayal can and does impact on how the broader public see the community, its struggles and its residents.

Eight: What the future holds

These questions give air to the broader socio-political and more specific practically oriented views of those whose voice(s) are most ignored and marginalised. Besides that though, the responses here can provide a firm basis upon which to show how the dominant media largely sidelines the positive side of community stories as well as individual and collective endurance, sacrifices and emotions, which would allow for more human and universalist connections.

We developed the eight categories above, with regard to the specific and contextual struggles experienced by each of the three communities, but also according to the principles of voice(s) outlined in chapter 1. These include the principle that voice is not static but is rather an ongoing process: narratives can change and develop over time. Voice is socially grounded, and as such can only be properly understood by placing it within its associated historical and political context. Each voice is distinct because each narrator is different, and each narrative is related to an interweaving set of related stories. There is never only one voice speaking to any particular set of events or issue, but a multiplicity of *voices*: the task for us as researchers and journalists is to seek out this multiplicity instead of hearing only the 'loudest' voice. Above all, we operated according to the fundamental principle that all voice(s) and every voice has value.

3

Glebelands Hostel, Durban

Dale T. McKinley

An integral part of the backbone of the apartheid migrant labour and influx control system was the establishment of single-sex hostels in the main urban centres of South Africa. Such hostels were essentially worker dormitories, often multi-storey and made up of small rooms (with common ablution areas), each of which usually housed many individuals. Like so many others around the country, the Glebelands hostel complex, located next to South Durban's Umlazi township, became the home of male workers who were brought in from the rural areas to fill mostly low-skilled and low-paying jobs in manufacturing and heavy industries (Zulu 1993).

From the beginning, the entire hostel system provided fertile ground for individual and collective, as well as ethno-political, conflict. The main means of someone getting a room in a hostel tended to be largely 'through personal contacts, or via companies', which 'contributed to the formation of homeboy [regional] cliques among residents in hostels'. The long-term result was that hostel social life tended to be 'organised around regional or ethnocentric arrangements' (Zulu 1993: 4). Initially run and managed by provincial authorities, the Glebelands hostel, similar to all others in Durban, has been administered by the eThekwini Municipality since the late 1990s.

On the political side, the hostel (historically an African National Congress [ANC] stronghold) saw intense conflict between the ANC and the Inkatha Freedom Party (IFP) during the early 1990s. The first official recording of a political killing was the gunning down of Dome Wellington Ngobese, the chairperson of the IFP branch at the hostel, in July 1992 (SAHA 1992). In the late 1990s, there was a shift to intra-ANC conflict when 'dozens of residents were murdered', followed by a lengthy period largely free from political violence until 2008 'when there were attacks on, and evictions of, people who joined COPE [Congress of the People]' (De Haas 2016).

As will be told in much more personal and direct detail below by the interviewees, the last five years have been a period of unrelenting violence and conflict, warlordism, and ethnicised and factionalised party politics, which have seen more than 100 residents being killed. All this has been accompanied by a seemingly never-ending cycle of mismanagement, corruption and criminality emanating from local government and the police.

Presently, the hostel houses an 'estimated 22 000 people living in approximately 80 blocks', most of which are extremely overcrowded and in serious need of repair, although there are a few 'newly constructed family units'. Unlike during the apartheid and early post-1994 years, a large number of residents now consist of families with a considerable majority being unemployed. As a result, poverty is rife, with the average income being an estimated R1600 per month and each adult resident supporting, on average, an estimated six other people (Gift of the Givers/Ubunye 2015).

INTERVIEWEES AND THE INTERVIEW PROCESS

All of the Glebelands residents who were interviewed have been, either directly or indirectly, at the forefront of ongoing collective and individual struggles to halt the violence and killings, expose corruption and mis-management as well as to seek justice for many of those who have been killed over the last several years. Two of them were previous leaders of the hostel residents' organisation (Ubunye bama Hostela or Hostel Unity), another two previously lived in blocks associated with hired killers, several have been personally threatened and/or targeted and all have lost either close friends or family to the ongoing violence and killings.

The resident interviewees are of varying ages but all are adults and the majority are middle-aged, male and originate from the Eastern Cape. Almost all have children (although in most cases the children are not residing with them at the hostel) and some still have partners, while others' partners have been the victims of the Glebelands killers. Half of the interviewees are formally employed, all in low-skilled and low-paying jobs.

Only one of the interviewees is not a hostel resident. Vanessa Burger is a long-time community and human rights activist, who has been the mandated public face of the Glebelands struggles since 2014. She has worked with and actively supported both Ubunye bama Hostela and those Glebelands residents who have been involved in the struggles described earlier. A few months before the interviews, she relocated away from Durban because of persistent harassment, the targeted theft of her vehicle, as well as numerous threats of physical harm.

Due to the extremely vulnerable and dangerous situation in which the resident interviewees find themselves, all of them requested to remain anonymous for fear of possible exposure. This is understandable given that at Glebelands such exposure has most often led to violent victimisation or retribution and, in many cases, death.

A timely reminder of this was provided during the interview process when the schedules had to be shifted because of threats of violence against some of the interviewees. The interviews that took place on the hostel grounds were conducted under very stressful conditions, while another interview had to be conducted at an undisclosed location because the interviewee was in hiding due to persistent death threats. Most of the interviews were conducted in English but in two cases there was the need for on-site translation.

THE PERSONAL SIDE

Listening to Glebelands residents speak about personal matters, their feelings, their emotions, their families, their fears and their challenges is a humbling experience. There is no better way to make a human connection with and try to better understand those who often appear to the general public, through the lens of the dominant media, as largely faceless actors, occasional victims and very seldom as ordinary people.

And yet, during the interviews it also became clear that most residents were extremely cautious about engaging in a more detailed conversation related to their personal lives. Upon reflection, such reticence made sense: the product of a combination of justifiable concern and fear about being identified, alongside negative views about how they have been portrayed in the dominant media.

When asked to describe daily life at Glebelands, a 30-something-year-old mother of three, whose husband was murdered at Glebelands for speaking out against corruption, had this to say:

> It is too tough. Things are terrible since [my now deceased] husband was busy building [a] home in [the] rural areas so everything now is stuck because [I am] not working … [and] most of the children are still young, they have to go to school, there are so many things, yes like school fees, shoes. I sell small things, just for baking, selling … chips, drinks. Life is difficult; it's very, very difficult (G5 interview).

For one of the elders of the community who is no longer able to find formal work, it is the widespread criminality that has accompanied the violence which makes it hard to even engage in survivalist work: '[Because of the violence/killings] it's hard even to sell now to go door to door selling peanuts, go door to door selling T-shirts and everything, because that is the way of doing things here. Even to go look for a R10 job, it's hard because if they can see you working here they will wait for you' (G4 interview).

One of the community's leaders, who has lived at Glebelands for over 20 years, provides an instructive reminder of the physical, psychological and social impact of living in an environment marked by almost constant disruption, violence and death:

> There are so many children here [who] drop out from school [and] the trauma people have here is worse than you can think. There are so many people who [have] died because … [of] the stress they had. And no one is prepared to come to you, to counsel you, nobody. Each and every time you take a step you think about death. I'm from town now but you know when I leave here I'm thinking oh am I going to reach there, once I reach there I feel happy but when I have to come back I have to think now am I going to reach my house? Because maybe someone is waiting [for] me somewhere … every minute, even if you are sleeping, [you] sleep like a bird in the tree (G2 interview).

Despite the resilience, grit and courage displayed by the vast majority of Glebelands residents, there is an acknowledgement of a distinct sense of powerlessness (but not hopelessness) in the face of the hostel's enduring bloodletting. In this case, in the words of a younger man whose attempts to serve on a peace committee have been met with constant death threats and have caused him to flee from one hostel block to another:

> It [the violence/killings] affect[s] me a lot, but there is nothing I can do, because I have to work for my kids. I can't run away from here because there will be no one to see me if I'm still alive and protected. We are like in a place where … there is no one to help us. We don't have powers. If we had powers I think this violence [would be] gone from here, that is my belief (G3 interview).

HISTORY AND CONTEXT OF THE AREA

One of the main reasons why those who watch, listen and read the dominant media often struggle to gain any meaningful understanding and appreciation of poor communities in struggle is because of the paucity of associated history and context. All the more so for a community such as Glebelands where, as will be shown in chapter 6, the coverage of the dominant media has almost exclusively focused on specific acts or events of violence and killing.

Such history and context is not simply the preserve of the 'expert' researcher, the academic or government officials and local politicians. Rather, it is greatly enriched when it encompasses the knowledge and views of the very people who live in and work with those respective communities. Here, Burger gives some useful insights into the institutional and socio-political history of hostels themselves, which provides a foundational backdrop to Glebelands' more contemporary realities:

> There are common issues at all the hostels and the biggest problem is political interference, manipulation ... what you would call favouritism, you know ward councillors or the hostel superintendent that would say favour a certain group who were supporters of a certain [political] party. When Ubunye bama Hostela came about it was to address social issues, service delivery issues, non-political stuff, but at the same time they couldn't move beyond the politics because the politicians themselves were too involved in using the hostels as power bases, exactly as the apartheid regime had done. So that tendency has followed through unchanged, and a lot of the ... power structures that existed then have continued even up till now (G1 interview).

In this light, it becomes easier to grasp the continuity between apartheid and post-apartheid politically motivated and ethnically oriented conflict that took place in hostels such as Glebelands. As the community leader interviewee details, the conflict and violence related to IFP–ANC turf wars and competition of the early to mid-1990s, returned in 1997 in the form of ethnic-related violence and conflict between Xhosa and Zulu members of the ANC. That round of violence only ended in 1999 after peace talks. And then there was renewed and similarly framed conflict in 2008, resulting in several deaths and hundreds of evictions when the ANC experienced a split that led to the formation of COPE (G2 interview).

COMMUNITY ORGANISATION

Unlike many other poor communities facing a range of local governance and socio-economic challenges, as well as problems centred on political party factionalism in the post-1994 period, Glebelands has not had a formally constituted and structured community organisation for the majority of that time. Rather, in the first 20 years of the democratic era, the dominant organisational space was taken up by two distinct areas of activity.

The most organic and democratically constituted were the block committees, which had been formed long before 1994. Every hostel block had a block committee. Among other administrative duties, the committees acted as something akin to 'security mechanisms to resolve internal conflicts within each block' and, importantly, to oversee and manage room allocations. 'Hostel rooms are inherited usually so ... the block committees were instrumental in preventing outsiders from coming in and exploiting the situation' (G1 interview). What is absolutely crucial to understanding the story of Glebelands is how and why the block committees were at first destabilised, then physically attacked and, finally, politically and practically undermined by being cast (with the dominant media playing a major role) as central – through the selling of beds – to much of the violence and conflict over the last several years.[1]

The remainder of the organisational space was taken up by political party branch activity, contestation and the activities of local and provincial party leadership, particularly the councillor. As has already been chronicled above, this area has always been dominated by one political party, the ANC, whether in unity or division.

What emerges clearly from the interviewees is that the block committees, despite their weaknesses and problems, were by far the most representative and democratic community structures in the hostel complex and the most effective at maintaining administrative as well as social cohesion. As one of the interviewees put it: '… to keep law and order, it's essential you have a community-based structure that is elected by the community and the block committees were. People [were] nominated as needed' (G1 interview).

Regardless of the fact that some members of the block committees 'got involved in selling beds themselves … this is an issue that has been common in all the hostels since before '94; it's petty corruption. If there had been a functioning administration and a functioning police force, the issue of bed-selling could have been easily stamped out, but there was no trust with the community, there was no outreach by the powers to resolve the situation, and a lot of them capitalised on it' (G1 interview).

Where the political party divisions and machinations began to substantively impact on the block committees was after the 2008 split in the ANC, the formation of the break-away party COPE and the subsequent widespread opposition to Robert Mzobe's ascension to the positions of ANC branch chairperson and local councillor. Things 'really came to a head [because] the main people who were leading that [opposition] and a lot of the defectors [to COPE] were block chairmen and committee members and they were also some of the main mobilisers against Mzobe' (G1 interview). In the period that followed, a large number of the block chairmen and committees were violently attacked and evicted from their resident blocks, with those aligned to Mzobe and the triumphant Jacob Zuma faction within the ANC taking control of many of the block committees and effectively splitting the Glebelands community both physically and along thinly disguised political party and ethnic lines.

It was more or less at this point that many residents, both at Glebelands and others hostels in the Durban area, began to search for alternative forms of organisation, voice and representation. 'The communities themselves were sick of fighting, they wanted to have peace, they were tired of being used, on both sides, so they had a lot of meetings … this is where Ubunye came about originally, to try and counter this and to try and bring people together, to unite the different hostels so they could speak with one voice' (G1 interview).

By 2013, Ubunye bama Hostela had been formally constituted; its very presence a testimony to the desire and ability of hostel residents to overcome historic and ongoing organisational, political, ideological and ethno-linguistic divisions. Initial programmes, even without any meaningful financial resources at hand, centred on efforts for hostels 'to develop their own sort of cooperatives' as a practical means 'to counter the [widespread] unemployment' and to develop the capacity to 'look after their own hostels' (G1 interview). Additionally, Ubunye 'tried everything … to deal with the violence. We wrote several letters [to the] Humans Rights Commission [with] nobody responding; IPID [Independent Police Investigative Directorate] nobody responding' (G2 interview).

These democratically mandated and collectively expressed attempts to engender peace and practical empowerment of hostel residents were not only actively blocked by the municipality but were mostly ignored by the dominant media. Combined with the ongoing violence directed at Ubunye leaders and members, as well as the associated corruption and criminality from the ranks of local government and the police, the cumulative result was that by 2016 Ubunye had effectively ceased to exist at Glebelands. As a resident sardonically noted, '… we are not condoms [to be] thrown away [but] that is what they do' (G2 interview).

ROLE OF THE STATE

For the vast majority of communities, regardless of their political history, geographical location and socio-economic status, it is at the local level where the face of government is most visible and where its actions have the most impact. This certainly applies to Glebelands and even more so due to the fact that it is local government (in this case, the eThekwini Municipality) which has officially been running and managing the hostel complex for the last 15 years.

As has been the case with a large number of other poor communities when it comes to the provision of basic public services and infrastructure at the local government level (especially hostels, which have historically been the most neglected), many of the negative experiences of Glebelands have been well documented by Burger, especially in the independent online media publications, the *Daily Maverick* and *Elitsha*. Indeed, the general living conditions in the majority of the blocks is similar to that which applies in most poor township communities across the country.

This side of government's role and activity, however, is the 'easier' one to notice and to expose, precisely because government's service delivery failures have become so normalised in South African society, with the dominant media playing a sizeable role in that regard. However, the other side of that role and activity – the specific links between poor or non-existent service delivery and management, and government corruption, greed, criminality and conscious cover-ups – is regularly ignored and often hidden by news reportage. For the Glebelands interviewees though, they are very much two sides of the same coin.

Take the case of security-related infrastructure, on which tens of millions in public funds has been spent, much of it to outsourced private companies with questionable links to those in government (Ubunye bama Hostela et al. 2014). Such infrastructure has usually been publically presented, including by the dominant media, as practical confirmation of local government's positive and preventative response to the ongoing violence and killings. But, that is not how one of the community leaders sees and experiences it:

> There are people from the state that are making money out of blood … There is a fence surrounding us, what was this fence for? There are cameras here, there are so many people shot next to these cameras but I never heard not even one suspect that was arrested

just because of the footage of the cameras ... There are private security companies, we don't know what they are doing here, they are going up and down, doing nothing (G2 interview).

Even more damning is the claim by a resident, who was an integral part of the Glebelands peace committee set up to ostensibly try to halt the violence, that local government officials and politicians are themselves party to the violence and killings through either conveniently looking the other way or through conscious facilitation:

Our government knows something about this violence, I can assure that ... Before elections last year [2016] we were at the ICC [International Convention Centre], there was the mayor of Durban there [and] those kings of KwaZulu-Natal ... [Also], there was a member of the ANC that is ruling inside here [at Glebelands]. He said we must stop now until elections then after we can start killing people – in front of the mayor ... and nobody followed that. After [the] elections one of our peace committee members, Thobile Mazongono, was killed. That's where they started; as the days go [another peace committee member] was shot again ... (G3 interview).

Another activist resident says it more directly:

It's simple ... the government is involved [in the killings and violence]. We even went to the police station for the [peace committee] meetings [but] all those meetings just collapse [and] nobody goes again. [Then] there comes the premier who said, 'No, we will not allow any person to be murdered anymore', [and he] disband[ed] everything, no talks or anything. So from that time [the] killings started ... after I think about a year they called us again [and] we [told] them ever since the premier came and the disbanding [of] talks ... people are dying; [they] kept quiet. After a year we called

49

again [and] he said 'we are still investigating ... no we'll call you again.' [But] nobody called us again ... I've lost hope (G4 interview).

Despite the justified cynicism about government's claims and promises and its unwillingness to act accordingly, Glebelands residents are adamant that government remains central to addressing and eventually 'fixing' Glebelands' myriad crises: 'We are still asking the government to stop this nonsense that is happening here, we need government to confront the truth; the government must deal with this situation honestly' (G2 interview).

ROLE OF POLITICAL PARTIES

If one pays attention and listens, then it becomes clear that the historically contiguous (apartheid/post-apartheid) frame set out earlier created the platform for the more recent and more violent conflict and corruption. Just as in the past, at the centre of the consequent picture are the roles and activities of political parties; in the case of Glebelands, this mainly applies to the ANC.

Burger picks up the story at a crucial turning point. In 2008, the eThekwini mayor, Willies Mchunu, 'had a meeting and called in all the [ANC] ward councillors who had hostels in their wards and told them to start opening up [their] own small businesses ... so that [they] can benefit from the new hostel budgets ... of course a lot of them did and that blocked the community's own initiatives' (G1 interview).

In turn, this provided ample space for the kind of political party machinations that would catalyse further division, conflict and violence:

> [Robert Mzobe] became ward councillor ultimately by default [because] he became [the] ... leader of the ANC branch at Glebelands by default, when Thabo Mbeki was recalled and there was a lot of unhappiness. So ... the ANC branch there was in sort of disarray, they were divided because some of them were supporting Zuma, others

were unhappy about Thabo Mbeki's recall.[2] The people, who [eventually] defected to COPE, brought a vote of no confidence against him [Mzobe] and the branch executive committee. And since that time, that branch of the ANC has never been properly reconstituted, [including] all elections and the actual ward councillor's position himself in that respect … Robert Mzobe led a march on the people who happened to be all centred around Block R, these were all the COPE supporters, the dissenters, the people who were not happy with what happened in the ANC … apparently Mzobe used a lot of the SACP [South African Communist Party] members who have since come out and publicly stated that they were incited against the guys from the Eastern Cape, the 'clever Mpondos', and they were told that these people had betrayed the ANC. So, there was a lot of persecution of people from the Eastern Cape, non-Zulus and people who joined COPE; a lot of evictions, a lot of killings … (G1 interview).

One of the community leaders not only confirms the direct role of the ANC but also identifies Mzobe as the local ANC kingpin and link man for party-initiated and party-beneficial corruption:

[The] violence [started in 2009 after] COPE was formed and some guys decided to join COPE. [That was when] the ANC of Glebelands, this branch … decided to remove all the people that … had chosen to be members of COPE; they even said 'we can't live here at Glebelands with COPE'. We strongly believe he [Mzobe] is behind all of this violence. In fact some of the guys who were working together with him in 2009 have … told us the full story. Glebelands is a bridge for corruption because it's where all of them come to do some developments … Development here in Glebelands is one of … the root cause[s]. I mean, you know when there is a project carrying on in Glebelands obviously the violence will break out. In 2009 there were new houses … about to be allocated and the violence broke out (G2 interview).

Other residents fill in the story by revealing how things then radiated out to anyone seen as standing in the way of those who control and abuse the historical power structures. Soon after an early 2014 meeting at Glebelands attended by senior regional and local ANC politicians, during which the role of block committees was attacked, block chairperson Nqabile Fika was abducted, tortured and murdered:

> [He was] taken by the police ... at night time [and] he never came back. Ever since that time ... they say 'no they don't want the block committees'. There were some leaders of [these] things who we know ... one of them is a police guy staying around here [and] the councillor was involved ... You will find out [in] each block [they are] collecting about R140 000 ... and definitely as according to our understanding and knowledge, after they [have] collected money somebody [is] going to die ... They [are] collecting to come and kill us (G4 interview).

The 'collecting' refers to the practice by self-declared leaders and various assortments of corrupt political and criminal thugs of forcing hostel residents to pay them money. It is exactly the same practice as a local mafia.

One cannot understand the contemporary crisis of violence and death at Glebelands without understanding what has happened and continues to happen within and as a result of the subsequent activities flowing from the ruling and dominant political party. The residents of Glebelands, for their part, certainly understand this, in the most direct and practical ways.

ROLE OF LAW ENFORCEMENT AND THE COURTS

It is bad enough for those at Glebelands that both government and political parties have largely failed them in every conceivable way. It is, however, even worse, and more especially in a context of serious insecurity, violence and death, that the one public entity – the police – whose primary purpose is to serve and protect all of those who live and work in

South Africa, are mostly seen and experienced as an integral part of the systemic problems and crises at Glebelands.

No informed observer, activist or resident at Glebelands will deny that there are individual police personnel who are not engaged in corrupt activities, are not acting in concert with criminals and are not involved in the killings. Yet, at the same time, they will confirm not only that there are those individuals who are doing that but that such activity is the more direct and localised reflection of a much more widespread and indeed systemic crisis of and within the police.

Whether that is in respect of supplying hit men with the means to kill and taking care of those who do not cooperate:

> They [the police] know even the names of these people; they know the leaders of this thing. Do we think ordinary men like me can have a box of bullets? Where did those men get those bullets? They just got them last week … [and] a new gun. These guys got weapons, they not playing, they got weapons, so that is why we still think [the police are] behind all this. They just see the taxi coming past [and demand] R200. If the driver [doesn't] want [to comply], tomorrow you won't see them; he'll be dead (G4 interview).

Whether it is about how the police deal with and treat those against whom there is a strong case, as opposed to those who are eyewitnesses and/or blow the whistle:

> When the [police] are catching somebody [they] put [them] in the police station [but then] they take him out … I don't know what's happening. The police [are] not straight. [When they arrested me for] attempted murder I [stayed] about a week in the prison, but [for] other people [it] was easy to come out (G6 interview).

Or whether it is how the police have actively sabotaged basic evidence and investigations as a means of ensuring impunity:

[I am] surprised why it takes so long to arrest suspect[s]. Some people have been killed in front of the cameras, some have been killed in court … but no one is convicted.[3] [I] do not know why these laws are not applied because all of us are protected by the Constitution of South Africa (G5 interview).

THE DOMINANT AND OTHER MEDIA

As will become clear in the analysis of the dominant media's coverage of Glebelands, the vast majority of the coverage has only taken place over the last four years, and even more specifically the last two years. Other than confirming the generally proportionate relationship between coverage and the amount of blood spilt, it links directly to the accompanying views and experiences of the interviewees.

Given her role as the mandated media liaison and the understandable reticence of most Ubunye and Glebelands leaders, activists and residents to be publically identified, it is not surprising that Burger has a great deal to say about the various media outlets and journalists she dealt with over the last several years. A crucial point she makes in respect of the coverage prior to the 2014 start of the violent upsurge is that coverage was extremely limited. This was because 'a lot of reporters [were] too scared to enter the hostels … [resulting] in a lot of ignorance, a lot of misconceptions' (G1 interview).

Even after the body count started to pile up, however, the dominant media was largely absent:

[They] didn't take any notice of Glebelands for at least a year and a half. We struggled, we battled to get coverage, it was unbelievably frustrating, the most appalling atrocities were going on and we could not get the media interested. I was lucky because I already had a good relationship with some of the reporters here from when I had been working with the Umbilo Action Group [another community organisation in Durban] … it was only when they started listening and they started reporting that other outlets started getting involved. It was hard work … there was no one at Glebelands who had any contact with the media at all (G1 interview).

Besides that, though, it was what had been covered and how life at Glebelands had been portrayed that was, and largely remains, so upsetting to most residents. It 'was always negative … always about the violence, always about the bad living conditions … very superficial with no understanding of the real issues. It was never … stories about the why, or what the people were trying to do themselves, or their genuine concerns or anything like that'. In particular, says Burger, 'national media has been absolutely terrible', with hostels like Glebelands being 'seen as like the black newspaper-type story [not] … of mainstream white interest' (G1 interview).

Burger also notes that while 'those perceptions have changed a bit' and some local journalists, such as 'Chris Ndeliso from the *Daily News*, Lungi Langa from *isoLezwe* … know exactly what has been happening … they don't have the resources [and] the time or the space to develop stories'. This is combined with the problem of 'political interference' where 'articles [have been] dropped … or cut to shit'. Indeed, some of the journalists have told Burger directly that they 'can't report on this because that will be the end of [their] job' and that other stories most often take precedence because the focus of the editors is 'top level' (G1 interview).

While there is general agreement among the interviewees that overall media coverage is now better than what is was before, this is not because they believe that the dominant media has developed a consistent conscience or realised the inherent worth of all people's lives. Further, there remains an enduring and justified scepticism around the willingness of the dominant media to delve into the more specific roles and activities of the government, political parties and the police.

In the words of the community leader: 'Most of the time in fact they say the root cause of this violence [is] corruption, which was done by the block committees, the selling of beds. From the beginning the media were using that false information … I think the problem of the media … some of them … [is that] they have contracts with the government you know, [so] they can't fully criticise government' (G2 interview). For another resident, the frustration is palpable: 'We tried our best to speak to the journalists [but] the key points [do] not appear in the paper' (G3 interview).

WHAT THE FUTURE HOLDS

Given the horror and tragedy of what has transpired at Glebelands for such a long time, there is a deep-rooted cautiousness about either making another set of demands for practical change or proclaiming any sustained progress in dealing with the long-standing and very real causes of the marginalisation, conflict and violence. As Burger wryly, but so accurately, notes, Glebelands 'is a microcosm of what's happening in South Africa. Unfortunately, because it is so awful and in your face … that has turned people off paying attention to it' (G1 interview).

Even so, while describing the present situation as 'very bad', one resident still acknowledges that 'we need help … we need government to give us support [and] we need the police … [but] we [will wait and see] how they carry on' (G6 interview). Similarly, it makes sense for residents, even in the face of serious repercussions, including death, to give continued voice to the struggle for their basic needs, for the essentials of a dignified life. For the mother of three young children, 'happiness' would be 'if the buildings, including the rooms, where we stay can be renewed and made for the family … like [fixing] leaks from the water pipes, sewerage [and] windows'. Maybe then her children would not 'get sick [or suffer from] diarrhoea, rashes …' (G5 interview).

Perhaps most tellingly of all, however, what shines through the thick fog of almost unimaginable fear, trauma, betrayal and all-encompassing violence is a fortitude of the human spirit and an indomitable sense of collective equality and justice, which are all so desperately needed:

I see hope because there [are] a lot of people who [are] supporting us … they [are] starting to see now what's going on. I can tell them the truth because there is nothing to hide on our side. Because South Africa is a free country, there must be no one who is scared to come inside to Glebelands … people must come and stay here. I can give them hope, I still have hope, I can't leave hope. At the end of the day the truth will come out (G3 interview).

4

Xolobeni, Eastern Cape

Dale T. McKinley

There are few places in South Africa, or for that matter globally, that are as beautifully wild and natural as Pondoland. It is the area in which the Amadiba Administrative Area is situated and within which Xolobeni is the largest village. Pondoland is the traditional territory of the Mpondo people, one of the isiXhosa-speaking peoples of South Africa, and it is situated on the south-eastern coast of the Indian Ocean in the Eastern Cape Province. It lies between the Mthatha and Mtamvuna rivers in the form of a coastal strip that is about 50 kilometres wide (SAHO 2013).

Pondoland has a long and complex political and social history. Depending on the historical source, the timeframe during which the Mpondo people settled in the area varies but suffice to say that by the sixteenth century they were well entrenched (Encyclopaedia Britannica 2017). After many wars, land conflicts and treaties signed with both the Dutch/Boers and then the British during the eighteenth to nineteenth centuries, like almost all black-owned and -settled land across South

Africa, Pondoland was placed under the administration of white colonial authorities with the passage of the 1913 Natives Land Act. Under the Bantu Authorities Act of 1951, the area was incorporated into the new apartheid 'homeland' of Transkei, which was the first such Bantustan to be granted 'self-government' by the apartheid regime (SAHO 2011).

During the late 1950s and early 1960s, the population of the area rose up in what has become known as the Pondoland revolt (or Nonqulwana in isiXhosa) (see Mbeki 1964). The uprising, with many African National Congress (ANC) supporters at the forefront, was in direct response to the forced imposition of tribal authorities allied to the apartheid regime and also against the impending self-government for the Transkei Bantustan (TRC 1998). While the revolt was violently suppressed, the area of Pondoland remained largely undeveloped throughout the apartheid era and has remained so since the democratic breakthrough in 1994.

Besides its unique history of land ownership, where land continues to be communally owned under the overall stewardship of local traditional governance structures (inclusive of a royal family, chiefs, headmen and headwomen, and traditional councils), the region is a biodiversity hotspot called the Pondoland Centre of Plant Endemism. With close to 200 known endemic species, it is South Africa's second-richest botanical reserve (Olalde 2017).

In the late 1990s, an Australian mining company, Mineral Resource Commodities (MRC), identified the red sand dunes extending for several kilometres along the coast in the Xolobeni/Amadiba region 'as among the world's 10 richest reserves of ilmenite, the ore that contains the metal titanium'. Thereafter, MRC, through its South African subsidiary, Transworld Energy and Minerals, and local partner, the Xolobeni Empowerment Company (XOLCO), applied for mining rights (Pearce 2017). Almost simultaneously, the parastatal responsible for the management, maintenance and development of South Africa's national road network (the South African National Roads Agency Limited, SANRAL) revealed plans to expand the main coastal highway (known as the N2) by cutting through the area and making it a toll road.

Immediate and active opposition to both of these processes by the vast majority of the Xolobeni/Amadiba community set the scene for what has since become a long-running conflict. This clash has involved the community, MRC, relevant government (national and provincial) departments and SANRAL, and at times there has also been conflict within the community itself. The main organisation that has come to spearhead the struggle against mining, as well as the toll road, is the Amadiba Crisis Committee (ACC), which was officially formed in 2007.

INTERVIEWEES AND THE INTERVIEW PROCESS

For this chapter, a total of nine people were interviewed at their homes, which are spread out across all five villages in the Xolobeni/Amadiba area. Most of them come from families who have lived in the area for generations, were themselves born and raised there and have lived there all their lives. Given that the population of the area has a large majority of adult women, it is not surprising that six out of the nine interviewees reflect that demographic. A majority of those interviewed are in their thirties and forties and have a sizeable number of children.

All of those interviewed are, in one way or another, involved in the struggle against the mining and the toll road and are all active citizens within their community. Several are elected leaders in the ACC, one is a ward council member and another is a member of the tribal council. None of them have formal, permanent jobs; everyone lives off and works the land as subsistence farmers, and two of them work with the local ecotourism project on behalf of the community. A majority of the interviews were conducted in isiMpondo (a combination of isiXhosa and isiZulu) with an on-site translator; the remainder were in English.

A striking feature about those who were interviewed and the community in general was their welcoming attitude and enveloping friendliness. Despite the fact that the research team were outsiders, visiting Xolobeni/Amadiba for the first time and did not speak isiMpondo, we were treated with the utmost respect and courteousness.

A specific incident was particularly instructive: having stepped outside one of the homes to take a quick break in between interviews, a dog that had recently given birth to a litter of puppies took fright and proceeded to give me a very deep and nasty bite on my ankle. On hearing my admittedly loud scream of pain, the homeowner and first interviewee, Nonsisa Mbuthuma, rushed outside, repeatedly apologised, wrapped my ankle in a cloth and reassured me that her dogs had just been vaccinated for rabies, thanks to a recent SPCA visit in the area. Even though I was feeling very sore, I left with a smile on my face because the overall experience reaffirmed my belief in people's innate goodness.

The other common attribute of all the interviewees was an abiding love of and personal connection to their land and the collective, democratic forms of land ownership. Linked to this is a deep pride in and appreciation of the social and political history of Pondoland, and more especially of sustained resistance. Combined, these qualities provide a formidable foundation for not only a socially strong and healthy community but also for collective action against those who would try to subvert the community's control and management of their land and way of life.

All of this is best captured by community leader and ACC spokesperson Nonhle Mbuthuma:

> I was raised by my grandfather [and] he told me that during the Pondo revolt the reason for them [to] sacrifice their lives to fight and people being killed [was] because land is so important. Once you have given up the land, you [have] lost your identity, you [have] lost who you are, you have nothing … you are like a dead person. If you want to be a good person, just protect the land, that's the resource you can inherit to your next and the next and the next. He always said that you cannot compare the money to the land because the money you can inherit to your child but the next generation cannot benefit, but the land it can benefit 100 generations if you take care (X1 interview).

The same strong feelings about the land and its centrality to understanding both individual and community stories came across when each interviewee was asked to provide some personal background. Nonsisa Mbuthuma (no direct relation to Nonhle) described her role as being 'to plough sweet potatoes because [we] want to protect this land. If [we] don't use this land they [are] going to take this land away. I know exactly I can't go anywhere; the only thing that makes me survive is the land' (X2 interview).

For Luthiwe Dimane, the relationship is one of directly mutual, practical benefit: 'This land is special to me because I [do] everything that I want to do ... like growing crops to feed my family, and also because I don't have a job ... [I] use this land to take them to school and also feed them; that's why to me it's very special' (X5 interview).

Another crucial fact that emerges from the sharing of personal stories is that very few of the interviewees have ever travelled far from Pondoland. While this might seem negative to a relatively highly mobile and urbanised South African population, in Xolobeni/Amadiba it is not seen that way at all. As will become clearer in other sections of the story, it is rather viewed as a confirmation of how life is much better experienced and enjoyed in this community; how fortunate residents do not have to deal with all the social and economic problems in other far-off places.

Sibusiso Mqadi captures this well in his recollection of an adolescent experience, which went on to shape his attitude towards mining and led to his involvement in the ACC struggles:

> When I was at school ... there was a trip that we took [to] Richards Bay Minerals to learn about the economics there and then I saw that kind of a mine. I spent three weeks there doing a learnership ... if you open the tap the water is like [the] colour of a spirit. And then there is a truck selling water, 20 litres of water at that time was R35 because this water is for washing [and] to drink. I know everything there ... this is not a life (X9 interview).

HISTORY AND CONTEXT OF THE AREA

In Xolobeni/Amadiba history matters; everyone is clear that if you do not know the history then you cannot even hope to know and understand the content and character of the contemporary conflicts and struggles in the area. As was evident from the start of each interview, that history is largely defined and shaped by the community's struggle to maintain their own forms of ownership and control over their land and to protect their chosen way of life. It is within and through this history that the present-day Xolobeni/Amadiba community defines itself and its relationships with those who would seek to change the ways of the community and their land.

Xalega Nobuhle puts it this way: 'This land is [the] same like this house; if you can come and say get out of this house, I just say no because this is my house. As a woman I'm not fighting for this land for only myself … I want my child to own this land … I want my son to live this life as the same as I live here' (X4 interview). And, in the words of Nonhle Mbuthuma:

> We are different than other communities in terms of culture … where there is no culture that's where people destroy nature. Here people they just respect nature and secondly the way of living you can see people know each other, you can walk from these five villages, they know all of them, but once you bring [that] kind of development … they don't even know their neighbours [and] that means Ubuntu [common humanity] is dead. We [take] care of each other; that is so important. And also the agriculture that we practise because in other places people are dependent [on] the government, here they are not dependent [on] anybody. Sharing is so important, that is the difference, but once those values [have] disappeared, you see Ubuntu [has] disappeared as well (X1 interview).

It is within this larger historical tableau that the more contemporary stories of the community's struggles against the proposed mining operations as well as the construction of the N2 highway are told. Thus, when MRC first tried to sell the mining idea to the community in the late 1990s and then again in the early 2000s on the basis that it would lift the community out of poverty, it was the community elders who reminded them that 'we are not poor … we have land, we have livestock, we have everything [so] please leave us alone, we don't need your project here, it's not good for us' (X1 interview).

Yet, rather than just pack up and leave, MRC began to engage in the tactic of 'outsiders' with money and power trying to divide the community by co-opting and buying people off. As Luthiwe Dimane relates, MRC then organised a community meeting at Komkhulu (the community/tribal council hall) where they told residents that they needed to form a committee, which would then 'work together' with the MRC and 'be a bridge from the community [to] that company'. Even though the community went on to 'elect that committee and have some meetings … we noticed that in this committee there [are] members that look like they earn something [and] it's where the conflict started. They form[ed] XOLCO in this way' (X5 interview).

Crucial to the overall story is what happened next. After MRC offered to take a community delegation to Richards Bay Minerals in order to see the benefits of a mining project, about twenty community members were elected and proceeded to go on the trip sometime in 2003. Luthiwe Dimane picks up the story:

> Mr Caruso [MRC boss] took those members [to] Port Shepstone to the expensive clothes shop to buy some suits, and after that they [gave] them about R500 pocket money and then they took them to Richards Bay. (One of the delegates) … a guy was called Scorpion said, no stop, this is not going to work in our community, because Scorpion thought that Mr Caruso [was] going to take them straight to that mine but [he took] them to the offices and played the projector [and also] didn't allow him to go and talk to the community [or to see] the livestock. Those members … they came back with different views … [those] people [who had] already been bribed [and] those ones [who] were fighting. When the meeting started

at Komkhulu, Scorpion [took] that pocket money and [said] that 'I cannot sell my land with R500' … It's when [there was] a split of the community, as it is until now (X5 interview).

Unfortunately for the larger community, some of the key people who chose to take the money, side with MRC, and become part of XOLCO, were also the ones who were put in charge of running what was becoming a successful community ecotourism project (X7 interview). At the time the project consisted of a camp, a lodge and a range of outdoor activities.

The people running the ecotourism … the director was Mr Qunya … were the people who were pushing the mining issues. So the issue was to make sure that they … do away with ecotourism. The office at Wild Coast Sun called Amadiba Adventures … was burned [in 2005/2006] [on] purpose … All the money … disappeared because they [were] trying by all means to finish the tourism project … We [tried] to open the case but the problem was that we didn't have evidence because everything was burnt there (X5 interview).

These early examples of corrupt, violent and criminal behaviour were added to by the murder of community leader Madoda Ndovela who 'was shot dead at his house … during the day. It was clear for us [that] the reason why he [had] been shot [was] because he was strongly, strongly opposing [the mining, more] than anyone else' (X1 interview). Also, in an early sign of how government and the police would respond, there was neither any meaningful investigation into Ndovela's murder nor any serious attempts by government to intervene and address any of the underlying issues.

A few years later in 2008, the government tried to unilaterally force the community to accept their granting of a mining licence to MRC, Transworld and XOLCO. Like MRC earlier, they did so through a combined and crude attempt to intimidate and effectively bribe the community. Nonhle Mbuthuma provides another part of the story that needs to be told in detail:

We just saw a huge tent … it was pitched close to Xolobeni school. When [we] go to Komkhulu … we ask what's that tent for? And they said the tent is for the social grant, those people who are going to apply for social grants and the IDs and government is trying to bring the services [to] where the people are. And then all of us were smiling and we [were] happy. I think the day after … I [got] a phone call from the journalist from *Umhlobo Wenene* … a radio [station] in Mthatha. They said are … you aware that tomorrow the minister of minerals and energy is coming to your place to grant a licence? You can imagine … you just heard from the media that the minister is coming to grant, but as a community … you are not even aware that there is an application. And then we go to the venue and when we arrived there it was packed, you know thousands and thousands, but the people where the mining is going to happen they were not even invited … not even one village was being transported to the venue, not even one.

When we entered we saw there was police like I never seen in my life, it was like Marikana. And there [were] helicopters … security was so tight. Then we go to the programme director as a crisis committee and we ask can we be on the programme … The executive mayor said that if you are not on the programme you are not invited. And then we just take a stand … and we said okay let's make chaos. We start singing, and when the minister tried to address the people … we start singing, we throw the apples to the minister to disturb and to make sure that nothing is happening. Then the executive mayor [goes] to the loudspeaker and tells the police, police please arrest all these people, put them in vans and just lock them there, we are busy here. And then the police they just become divided … because some are from here in Pondoland and … a station commander [who] said no I can't arrest people when they [are] fighting for their own rights … The meeting was disrupted completely and the minister couldn't continue; she just left [along with] the people who had been transported … from PE [Port Elizabeth], Mthatha you know all the other towns (X1 interview).

It is these kinds of historical and contextual details that never make it onto the pages or broadcasts of the dominant media, regardless of the fact that they are absolutely essential to any understanding of what has transpired and why. As a classic example, when Nonhle Mbuthuma says that those who are on the 'pro-mining side' are 'not the community' but simply a 'group of business people [who] are looking for money in this mining thing' (X1 interview), it is not just her personal opinion but a statement of fact, which can be supported by the historical record.

Likewise, she points out that the struggle over the N2 toll road has followed a similar path of using carrots and sticks and trying to sow division and confusion within the community. 'It's been so many years going back and forwards. If they see … it's difficult to push the mining, they push the N2. If it's difficult to push the N2, they just push the mining. The [initially] proposed road was not along the coast [but] far inland, and they change it to make sure it's more along the coast … closer to the mine, that is why we totally oppose the N2 toll road' (X1 interview). And finally, when she notes that several powerfully connected people, such as the former director general of the Department of Minerals and Energy, Sandile Nogxina, high-flying ANC-allied lawyer Maxwell Boqwana and the daughter of Bizana Municipality's mayor, are directly involved with XOLCO, the framing of the Xolobeni/Amadiba conflict and struggle becomes much clearer.

COMMUNITY ORGANISATION

The history of Pondoland is also a history of organised resistance and struggle, but it is one that has been driven by specific events and actions, which have often divided and created conflict within the communities in the area. In other words, besides the long-standing cultural organisations and structures of institutional (traditional) authority, there has rarely been a more permanent or sustained organisation over a long period of time that could be said to represent the vast majority of the community.

Thus, during the first few years of MRC's presence and activity in Xolobeni/Amadiba, alongside SANRAL's manoeuvrings around the N2 toll road, the community sought to engage MRC, SANRAL, local and national government, as well as those within the community who wanted mining to take place, through the auspices and channels provided by the tribal council. However, precisely because the historic role of the council is not to take any sides in an individual or collective/community conflict but rather to act as a neutral arbiter, the reliance on the council did not fit the organisational needs of those in the community who were against the mining and the toll road. This is why the ACC came into being.

ACC spokesperson Nonhle Mbuthuma gives this succinct version of its origins and purpose:

> We just decided okay, now we do have our tribal council but the role of the tribal council is for all of us even if you like the mining or you don't like the mining ... Now if they just take one side that means it's not the way they were designed for ... [So] we just sit down and say okay let's form a committee that is going to focus to fight against the mining. And then in 2007 that is where [we] formed the committee which is called the Amadiba Crisis Committee. And this committee is represented according to the [five] villages (X1 interview).

From its formation, it was clear that the ACC was the de facto community organisation for the entire Amadiba area. This was the case not just because it was well organised and had a coherent basis for its activities but because it was obvious to anyone (who was either paying attention at the time or who has subsequently actually talked with and listened to community residents) that the ACC was, and remains, representative of the vast majority of the community. As a member of the tribal council avers, once it was clear to the council that 'the people they say, no this is not for us ... then even the tribal authority are on the side of the people because the people they say that this is not good for us' (X6 interview).

While there certainly are some in the community who remain resolutely in favour of both the mining project and the N2 toll road, the fact is that they are relatively few in number. Further, available evidence points to their choices, especially in respect of the mining project, being heavily influenced by financial 'rewards' and work 'incentives'. On the other hand, for those who are ACC activists and members the main 'reward' awaiting them is potential attack and arrest – the key 'incentive' being a strong collective and community bond that binds them to a long history of love for the land and the bounties of nature.

It is that kind of connectivity and purpose that not only sustains the ACC but gives it an indelible strength and character. For ACC member Xalega Nobuhle, the ensuing loyalty is palpable: 'Even though you can give me [a] car to change my mind or to change to be a pro-mine, no I'm a crisis [ACC member] for life' (X4 interview). For another member, Fundile Madikizela, the connection is very real: 'There is a slogan … that you can kill a crisis member but still another one is being born today, maybe stronger than this one. So it doesn't matter, this is going to continue' (X7 interview).

ROLE OF THE STATE

There has always been a complicated and often conflictual relationship between the people of Pondoland and the various arms of the South African state. Even if differentially applied and experienced, such a relationship has cut across the apartheid and post-apartheid eras. At the heart of this is the general unwillingness of the people in this area to be materially and developmentally beholden to the state and to be told by government officials and entities at various levels what it is they can or cannot do with the land.

The basic sentiment of the Xolobeni/Amadiba community is succinctly captured by tribal council member Mabhude Danca: 'The government wants to rule or to own everything because they want everyone to depend on [them]. Here we are uncontrollable by the government' (X6 interview). And therein lies one of the most fundamental problems of any government in dealing with this community (and which in a linked way, also applies to the dominant media). Unless and until the government treats the community with respect and actually sits down, talks and listens to what kind of 'development' they desire, any government-initiated and/or-supported development will be seen as illegitimate and will be resisted.

Resident Luthiwe Dimane understands this in the most simple yet profound of (democratic) ways when it comes to the mining story: 'The state and this Australian guy Mr Caruso [treated the] community [like we] are stupid … I [am] supposed to take a decision, not the people coming from outside …' (X5 interview). So, too, does Mabhude Danca: 'There is no role here for government … they didn't do anything for us. They [have been] trying to push us to the mining only [even though] here we ask to have the tourism project … they just take sides [with the mine] (X6 interview).

As many of the interviewees explicitly stated, even though they would very much like to have piped water, formal sanitation and electricity, the community has long since stopped believing in all the promises and is not waiting for government to 'deliver' these basic services. Nor is it willing to engage in trade-offs to potentially get them; in this case, by agreeing to the mining project and the construction of the N2 toll road. The community is far too experienced in knowing how government often operates as well as the compromised relationships and interests of those who stand to benefit.

A good example is the story told by ACC member and community activist Sibusiso Mqadi about how in the late 1990s Amadiba resident Zamile Qunya quit as the Bizana mayor and became the director of the community's flagship ecotourism project, Amadiba Adventures, at the time when it was generating significant income. Within a short space of time, most of those funds disappeared, and Zamile Qunya, with the help of his brother, Bashin Qunya (who was employed by the government as a manager in the Department of Tourism), morphed the tourism project into XOLCO. The end results were the destruction of the ecotourism project, directorships in XOLCO for the Qunya brothers and the planting of seeds of division and conflict within the community.

From this experience, it became clear to most residents that 'this Xolobeni mining is not local [and that] most of the people in government have their personal interests' (X1 interview). 'They care [about] only two project[s] because they know exactly that they [are] going to benefit. We

know government likes mining because they going to benefit something'
(X5 interview). 'The municipality is interested, the government is interested
[and yes] the police department are also part of this' (X7 interview).

ROLE OF POLITICAL PARTIES

Given both the historical and post-apartheid dominance of the ANC in
Pondoland in almost every aspect of institutional, government and general political life, there is little distinction between the ANC and the state.
In other words, what applies in respect of how government is seen and
experienced largely applies in respect of the same for the ANC.

During the week in the Amadiba area, not a single interviewee or
anyone else in the community made more than a passing reference to the
specific role and/or activities of the ANC; and none even once mentioned
any other political party. Even when the ANC was mentioned, it was in
very general and all-encompassing terms; indirectly confirming the view
of equivalency between government and the ANC.

Perhaps the experience of how an ex-ACC leader and now local ANC
councillor, Mzamo Dlamini, has become 'so busy' that the community
rarely sees him and how the ward he represents has seen little/no development (X9 interview) has helped frame these perspectives. This comment
by resident Xalega Nobuhle aptly sums up that view: 'The politician and
the government [are] not going to be on our side because first of all the
politicians are looking for their family and himself to benefit and also the
local government [are] looking [for] the tax profit' (X4 interview).

ROLE OF LAW ENFORCEMENT AND THE COURTS

Under normal circumstances, there is very little need for or contact with
the police in Xolobeni/Amadiba. This is for two main reasons: there is
hardly any criminal and/or otherwise illegal activity; and the nearest
police station is more than 30 kilometres away on poor dirt roads. The
same lack of accessibility applies to the courts.

The last 15 years in Amadiba has been anything but normal. From the moment MRC arrived in Pondoland and began its mining crusade, to when the police failed to identify and apprehend those who burnt down the ecotourism camp and stole most of its assets, and then did little to solve the murder of community leader Madoda Ndovela, thus did the overall relationship between the community and the police change dramatically. Unlike the narrowly time-bound focus of the dominant media on the police, precipitated by the assassination of Sikhosiphi 'Bazooka' Radebe, the community of Xolobeni/Amadiba have a much wider and more in-depth perspective.

A good representative example is given by Nonhle Mbuthuma about the time in 2007, just after the formation of the ACC, when they went to the police to report MRC and Transworld for what they considered trespassing and conducting illegal activities on their land (MRC was ostensibly conducting an environmental impact assessment without the knowledge of the community).

> All of us you know we asking ourselves what the hell is going on, you see my house … they were just drilling just here behind this room, and we were just taking the knobkerries and chasing them to say what the hell you doing! And they said no, we're just doing an environmental impact assessment … and you know it was a chaos. The police said thank you but they didn't do anything. And [then] we went to [the] municipality, also the municipality said thank you but they didn't do anything (X1 interview).

When ACC members destroyed the dust monitors that the MRC had installed in people's yards, the police were quick to deploy and carry out multiple arrests. Several ACC members were charged with vandalism and destruction of property but, as soon as the ACC secured legal representation, the charges were withdrawn.

In the following years, there have been a number of similar incidents. For example, in late 2015, after a pro-mining group had launched a series of violent attacks on ACC members and supporters, which included the fatal shooting of one ACC supporter, a case was opened with the police. Although the police subsequently arrested several suspects, they were released soon thereafter. At present, no one has ever been held responsible for this or any of the others deaths/murders that have occurred in Xolobeni/Amadiba (X2 interview; X4 interview).

The cumulative outcome is the ACC's belief that the police have effectively been captured by the various pro-mining forces both outside and within the state. 'When you talk about the police, you [are] still talking about the government that is involved in this mine ... because the police they [are] against the ACC ... they care about those people that want mining' (X6 interview). For another ACC member, 'those people that are killing ... it is a combination between those people, [the] police and the other departments with the mining company. That company ... it's very powerful to pay someone or bribe; [it] is nothing else [but] money' (X3 interview).

THE DOMINANT AND OTHER MEDIA

In an age where there is a constant flow of information and expanding communication technologies and media platforms, there is something unique about a place that remains largely removed from that world. On one hand, the relative geographical isolation, absence of readily available consumer goods and dearth of technological infrastructure means that the community simply does not have the means to access most of the media platforms or to make full use of the information highways that are generally available (even if not equally accessible) to others.

On the other hand, the isolation and lack of availability and access in many ways 'protects' the community from the harsh and often depressing world of constant (and regularly untruthful) information, competition and commentary. In doing so, it provides more space for the kind of organic, self-sustaining development and way of life that the vast majority of the community seeks to sustain. And that is why every interviewee, while acknowledging the desire, for example, to be connected to the power grid and to have better cellphone communication infrastructure has no parallel desire to see the kind of urbanised, atomised and conflictual ways of life and living that most often accompany one side of the spread of new information and technology.

Such contradictions frame the experiences and relationships of the Xolobeni/Amadiba community with the media. As Nonhle Mbuthuma relates, before the formation of the ACC, which opened up a whole new media terrain for the community, 'it was very rare [for] outside people to know because this is a remote area … we never heard of the [dominant] media, as we don't even read the newspapers, we just listen [to] the radio, we [are] not thinking that it can help, we just fighting the fight for ourselves' (X1 interview).

Even though the ensuring years have seen an increased presence and coverage, the community still remains largely cut off from the world of information, about which a younger Sibusiso Mqadi is quick to note: 'We [still] don't have access to media, all of us … because we don't have a signal first, no internet access, we don't have a television, paper...' (X9 interview). Most of the community, including ACC members, have had very little access to and contact with the dominant media. Rather, almost everyone gets their information from and has had occasional engagements with local or community media (specifically radio) as well as civil society organisations (CSOs).

Indeed, from 2007 it was through such CSO support that the ACC was able to access some of the dominant media outfits, which, in turn, led to national coverage of the conflict for the first time. This brought with it welcome public exposure in the case of the first national-level story, through the South African Broadcasting Corporation's environmental current affairs programme *50/50*. But it also brought to the fore fears within the ACC and the community that such exposure could lead to them being targets for violent attack, especially after the recent murder of Madoda Ndovela (X1 interview).

Once the dominant media began to occasionally and selectively cover the Xolobeni/Amadiba story, both ACC activists and community residents sought to access such coverage as much as was practically possible. In most cases, this happened through shared podcasts and videos with those who had access to smartphones or when people were able to purchase a newspaper during trips to nearby towns (X9 interview). As a result, many in the ACC and community were, for the first time, able to hear, read and assess what was being said about them and their struggles. For ACC activist Baliwe, what she heard and read was troubling:

> Sometimes [we see] on TV people that [are] not from here ... talking lies. Like the ministers and everyone from the media say [that] the people from Xolobeni are poor and they don't want development. But if you can come here ... the thing that you saw in the paper or the story that you read is different now because you are sitting with us, which means that is the way to send the information (X3 interview).

For others, the realities of editorial interference and/or censorship of individual journalist's initial coverage were brought to the surface, alongside the realisation that many of the journalists are themselves mostly ignorant of key aspects of the mining story:

> There's a newspaper [journalist who came to] a meeting last year at Komkhulu ... that journalist wrote the story [but] when they released the story it was not the same. We tried to call him and then he said the mistake is from the editors ... we trusted him and then the story. [Also] those people (some journalists) they didn't know [what was] going on here because even though we met them they just asking the question ... why you don't want mining because the mine is going to bring the job opportunities? [But] when you ask him or her do you know what kind of mine this is and then they said no; do you know how long it's going to operate there, no ... when you are trying to tell them ... they just [keep] saying hey we

didn't realise what this is, which means the media are not telling them the right story (X8 interview).

Even though the ACC and community are now more aware of the negative effects of misinformed, constructed and biased coverage by the dominant media, they also recognise that it has provided opportunities for them to engage more alternative, positive, informed and reaffirming media and information-sharing spaces. For example, while the dominant media gave extensive but mostly surface-level coverage of the assassination of Bazooka Radebe, this precipitated increased alternative and civil society related media attention and support.

WHAT THE FUTURE HOLDS

If there is one thing that is predictable about the Xolobeni/Amadiba community it is that they will never stop struggling for their land and way of life. Community resident Fundile Madikizela claims: 'This is going to continue. I feel we are getting … stronger. This is our land, so we fight for the land; we [would] rather die for our own thing' (X7 interview). Fellow resident and ACC activist Xalega Nobuhle concurs: 'They [are only] going to mine here if everyone is dead. As a community we are willing to die before they mine' (X4 interview).

But what also became clear in the interviews is that a significant part of that struggle is to contest the dominant societal and ideological narrative, often replicated and reinforced by the dominant media, which equates an activity such as mining with necessary and largely positive economic and social development. Inherent in this struggle is the affirmation of the community's right to say no and thus to be able to choose the content and character of desired development. As with so much in this community, the struggle for such proactive affirmation is understood and approached with past history in mind. In the words of Xalega Nobuhle: 'Before, [during] the apartheid government, as black people we didn't get that chance to say no or yes, but now we have power to say no' (X4 interview).

This crucially important component of the conflict and struggle in Xolobeni/Amadiba is best captured in practical terms by tribal authority council member Mabhude Danca:

> We need electricity and water and everything but the first one to develop this community is tourism … because the ecotourism [is] going to develop this community and also bring job opportunities for the youth. We don't like people thinking that we don't want anything … that is a lie. We are not here to say that we don't want any development, we need the development, but the only thing that we don't want is the mine (X6 interview).

Yet, the necessary prerequisite for there to be significant and positive movement towards the kind of development that the community desires is the defeat of the mining project. Through a combination of practical mobilisation and struggle, increasing domestic and international support, as well as a victorious ruling in the High Court that the state must seek prior and informed consent from affected communities before granting mining licences (a ruling that is being appealed by the Department of Mineral Resources), the ACC and community have to date prevented the granting and operationalisation of a mining licence.

The ACC is ready for whatever the outcome might be. As Nonhle Mbuthuma puts it: 'We [are] going to continue to fight, no matter what … we have our own ways of dealing with the issues here… at the end it's going to be in favour of us' (X1 interview).

5

Thembelihle Community, Johannesburg

Dale T. McKinley

In many ways, Thembelihle is an urban microcosm of the South African transition. As the shackles of the apartheid urban planning and influx control systems began to unravel in the early to mid-1980s, a small settlement 'was established on municipal-owned land' that was situated southwest of Johannesburg, adjacent to the predominantly Indian suburb of Lenasia. Its first residents were a combination of urban and rural migrants, alongside the 'employees of a brick manufacturing company' (SERI 2013) operating in the area.

It was soon given the name Thembelihle, which literally translated means a 'place of hope'. And, indeed, it was just that for the majority of its early residents who arrived for one or more very specific reasons: to look for work in the Johannesburg metropolis; to be closer to jobs and other amenities associated with the neighbouring Lenasia community; and/or to move away from parents and family to establish their own homes and families.

Although these initial 'residents were granted permission to reside at the settlement by the [apartheid] government and were given materials to construct informal dwellings' (SERI 2013), it remained classified as a 'squatter settlement'. This meant that despite its rapid growth throughout the late 1980s and early 1990s, basic services were not provided and little or no socio-economic development was undertaken by the apartheid authorities. By the time of the democratic elections in 1994, the residents of Thembelihle had managed to not only survive the brutalities of the apartheid system but also to make the area their permanent home. People lived in their own mostly self-built dwellings, however modest; children went to local schools; and most of those who had jobs worked nearby. In other words, Thembelihle had put down roots; it had become a real community.

Once the new democratic government was in place, the community fully and rightfully expected it to finally begin the process of providing basic services and faclitating other infrastructural and economic development in the area. However, very little of this was forthcoming, and in 1998 residents were told by local and provincial government that the entire community needed to be moved to a new area (Vlakfontein, several kilometres to the south) because Thembelihle was situated on dolomite and was therefore unsafe for residential upgrading or further development (McKinley 2002; Segodi 2018).[1]

As it turned out, although Thembelihle is indeed resting on dolomitic ground, so too is a sizeable portion of several residential areas in and around Johannesburg. Further, a July 1998 letter from the local government authority to a local developer, who had made an application for a housing development in Thembelihle, revealed the real reason behind the removal plan. It stated that 'it will be too expensive to develop the area for low income housing' and that 'the installation of essential services and the erection of houses will only be suitable for medium to high income beneficiaries' (McKinley 2002).

Ever since, there has been an unrelenting struggle by the community, which now consists of at least 8000 households (SERI 2013), to resist

forced removal and to be recognised as a formal settlement and community by government in order to receive basic services and to be eligible for
further financial assistance and economic development. At many points
in this journey, the conflict has turned violent and the state has become
particularly repressive. Although, at varying times, large numbers of
residents have been involved in these struggles, the main community
organisation that has led the way is the Thembelihle Crisis Committee
(TCC), which was formed in the early 2000s.

INTERVIEWEES AND THE INTERVIEW PROCESS

Interviews were conducted in the community with seven people, all
of them residents of Thembelihle and all living in shacks. One of the
interviewees has been living in the area almost from the time that the
settlement was initially established in the early 1980s, several have been
there for over 20 years and one was born in the community after 1994.

Five of those interviewed were males and two were females, with ages
ranging from a great-grandmother in her mid-seventies to a nineteen-
year-old young man. All but the two younger men have children (most
of them born in Thembelihle), one has grandchildren and several have
other (extended) family members staying with them.

A majority of the interviewees are activists in the TCC and everyone
has been involved, in various ways, with the community struggles against
removal and for basic services and economic development. All except
one are not formally employed (although several used to be employed in
the past). Most of the interviews were conducted in English with two of
them being conducted in a combination of English and Setswana (with
on-site translation where necessary).

THE PERSONAL SIDE

When it comes to a place like Thembelihle, the difference between per-
ception and description versus on the ground reality is extraordinary.

Most often perceived and indeed described, including in the dominant media, as an 'informal settlement' and even sometimes a 'squatter camp', full of dangerous people and a place to be avoided, Thembelihle and the vast majority of its inhabitants are anything but these things.

Besides visiting and spending some time in the community, the best antidote to such falsehoods is to sit and listen to the personal stories of residents and activists. Their telling includes many examples of incredible personal and family hardship and practical difficulties. But, they also tell a story of resilience and tenderness, enduring life skills, human connection, community spirit and relational warmth and love.

At the heart of the personal stories here is the connection between the place of living and the pursuit of a better life, be it at an individual, family or income/work-related level. Whether it is 72-year-old grandmother Cynthia, who arrived in 1995 from Soweto so that she and her husband (since passed) could have their own place to live (T3 interview); 40-something-year-old Ghetto Kopane, who also moved to the community in 1995 in order to find employment and start a family (T1 interview); or 43-year-old father of three, Bhayiza Miya, who left his nine other siblings because his father told him to strike out on his own (T4 interview) – almost everyone in Thembelihle reflects, in the most practical and personal of ways, the very name of the place itself.

Also central to most of the life stories is an incredible ability to adapt to changing and mostly difficult material circumstances in order to sustain oneself and family. Take the example of Ghetto Kopane, who was doing well for himself working at a garage in the first few years after his arrival but, like so many others in the 1990s, lost his job. With a new wife and two young children to support, he sought the counsel of his uncle who taught him 'to work with my own hands'. As a result, he has 'ended up doing [piece] jobs [like] building, painting [and] carpentry' to feed his family (T1 interview).

Although unemployed for the last 20 years, elderly Cynthia somehow continues to find a way to support two children and three grandchildren on her old-age government pension of R1600 a month (T3 interview).

Arguably the most heart-rending but ultimately triumphant personal story is that of 29-year-old Trevor Ntlatseng. Having arrived at the tender age of two with his mother and grandparents, Trevor was on his own with his two younger sisters and brother by the time he was thirteen; his mother having left the family when he was eleven and both his grandparents having passed away within the next two years. He picks up the story:

> I was staying here with my two sisters and a brother. I had to drop [out of] school, I had to go and look for a piece of bread which I must come and share with my sisters, so they can go to school. As a young man I … did feel like I was cursed, [like I was] nothing in this country. [But], I started working when I [was] thirteen years old. I was earning R15 per day [in] those years [helping] an Indian guy … I carried on working and said you know what, I'll get old then I'll go back to school because I can't leave what is giving me a piece of bread in the house because I'm the breadwinner alone. [But] I started … drinking alcohol. The day I regretted drinking alcohol is the day I was arrested for something which I never did. I stayed one year six months in Sun City [on a charge of attempted murder and robbery for which he was eventually acquitted]. I learnt my lesson and I said I'm done with alcohol. I started going [to] church … so from there it's where I am today [an intern at the local clinic through the government's Expanded Public Works Programme] (T6 interview).[2]

HISTORY AND CONTEXT OF THE AREA

Much like Xolobeni/Amadiba, although in very different historical, geographical and social/cultural settings, the core defining feature that has framed the life story of Thembelihle is the land. Indeed, the origins and subsequent growth of the community are a direct result of a general lack of available land for residential use by the poor in and around the Johannesburg metropolis – this traverses both the apartheid and post-apartheid eras.

Once the initial wave of people had erected their shacks, established a more permanent community presence and warded off the numerous attempts by the dying apartheid state to prevent the expansion of the settlement (T7 interview), there was an extended period of general peace (with the government of the day) and unimpeded growth that paralleled the early transition to democracy. However, this did not mean that the desire and practical need for more land as well as basic services receded; indeed, the opposite was the case.

While not representing a community-wide organisation, there were political party and civic activists in Thembelihle in the mid- to late 1990s who organised the community and engaged in mobilisation around demands for additional land as well as basic services, such as water. For example, a sizeable piece of land called 'Extension 17', which was close to Thembelihle on the back side of Lenasia, was identified. 'So they [the activists] said move us there across the road [but] it was a problem [for the authorities] … because [the land was] close to our Indian community … [the refusal] was class politics' (T4 interview).

When it came to services, there was some early success in getting the new African National Congress (ANC)-run Johannesburg Municipality to install communal water taps. However, because the taps were few and far between, demands were then made to extend the water pipes so that there could be taps in each shack yard. The government refused and the local ANC branch and councillor also actively opposed the initiative. So, active members of the community, including two of the interviewees (Bhayiza Miya and Siphiwe Segodi) helped to mobilise the community to lay and install the pipes themselves (T7 interview).

This was a hugely important and more widely symbolic act, not only of popular initiative and defiance but one that sent a message that the people of Thembelihle were there to stay. While it was completely ignored by the dominant media, it galvanised many of the activists and new community organisations were soon formed; one of them was the TCC. But it was also clearly viewed as a direct challenge to the power and interests of the ruling ANC, the local government it was running and some of its influential and wealthy backers in neighbouring Lenasia.

By late 2001, the municipal and provincial authorities announced that the entire community would have to be moved from Thembelihle to Vlakfontein due to the dolomite problem. Not surprisingly, the community refused and invited the authorities to sit down and talk with them. Instead, the notorious private security firm, Wozani Security (otherwise known as the Red Ants), was hired by the authorities to tear down shacks and thus forcibly remove the residents of Thembelihle, without any due process or legal sanction (McKinley 2002). In the event, the community successfully resisted, physically forcing the Red Ants to retreat and the authorities to abandon the eviction plan. In the words of Siphiwe Segodi:

> They made a blunder which united the community behind the TCC because when they tried to dismantle the shacks illegally … everyone felt threatened within the community and managed to mobilise behind the TCC. We shut down SA block [home to the ANC offices] and declared Thembelihle a no-go area for the councillor; he didn't come to Thembelihle for some time. I think [the successful mobilisation] also bolstered the community's confidence (T7 interview).

What popularly became known as the 'battle of Thembelihle', which did receive some media coverage even if almost wholly focused on the violent confrontations between residents and the Red Ants, kick-started what has now become a 17-year-long 'battle' for security of tenure, infrastructural and housing upgrades and the delivery of basic services. At the centre of the consequent struggles has been the TCC, which has become the most popular, respected and effective organisation in the community.

As will be seen when it comes to the analysis of media coverage, the TCC and the core struggles of the community that it has led cannot be understood if the sole or main focus is on the numerous protests and ensuing conflict with the police. Indeed, one of the most impressive, yet poorly captured and understood, characteristics of Thembelihle's struggle is the democratic, procedural lengths to which it has gone to try to engage the various levels of government, alongside its official representatives and the politicians involved. As TCC leader Bhayiza Miya relates:

> For us to go to the protest it's not that we sleep and then we dream about the protest, no, it's a continuation, it's a frustration that leads us to protest. From the writing of letters, memorandums … we follow the procedures. We deliver the very same memorandums … the petition [but] there [is] no response, no response [to] all the memorandums. [They] have never heeded any response or any occasion to say yes, we are busy with your call, with your memorandum or whatever you have brought to us. A lot of the Thembelihle struggle has been about petitioning the state to deliver services in particular here, to formalise this place (T4 interview).

Beyond the protests, mobilisations and engagements with authorities, however, there is a very real and practical sense of community in Thembelihle that is underpinned by a broad, collective embracing of everyone's right to dignity, equality and justice. This is one of the reasons why the TCC and the larger community have been able to wage a virtually uninterrupted struggle for such a long time. A long-time resident and TCC activist reminds us that 'this thing of South Africa in diversity … we are practising that here because there are people here from all sides of South Africa [and] even from Malawi, Mozambique, Somalia, Ethiopia, Namibia [and] Zimbabwe. We might differ in talking languages but there's love in this community' (T1 interview).

Betty, one of the older members of the TCC, speaks to this with strong emotion: 'I love Thembelihle. People here they [have] wonderful souls, they [are] working together … [the] people of Thembelihle, they've got good hearts … As Thembelihle we are a very strong community'

(T2 interview). A much younger Trevor Ntlatseng is quick to note that although 'Thembelihle, it means nice place, people don't take it that way, they just [think] … people who are staying here are violent, [that] they like violence … people they treat us like that, but we are not like that' (T6 interview).

COMMUNITY ORGANISATION

As mentioned above, from the initial formation of Thembelihle, there have always been various forms of organisation and mobilisation precisely because the community itself has never been officially recognised and treated as a permanent settlement. What this has meant is that for more than 30 years and despite the minimal measures (for example, mast lighting and communal water taps) undertaken by the post-1994 government, there has been both an objective and subjective need for the community to organise itself in order to simply survive as a community.

The contextual continuities are not lost on TCC leader Bhayiza Miya, who notes that the TCC's formation in 2001, a mere seven years after the democratic breakthrough, was confirmation that there was 'a continuation from the previous regime, a continuation of fighting an oppressive system'. Even if under different political conditions, Miya is clear that the core reasons for the existence of the TCC have not changed: 'the struggle is still the same from the old regime and the new regime' (T4 interview).

He is also clear about why the TCC has remained popular with and continues to be supported by the community, as well as why some of the controversial tactics adopted by the TCC have had positive practical outcomes. Here, the main example centres on the recent success in getting significant parts of Thembelihle officially and legally hooked up to the electricity grid.

> Thembelihle people are clear about this … the electricity [and] the services that we are getting in Thembelihle never came because the ANC likes us. No, it's because we stood up and said we'll fight them,

we'll even connect ourselves to the Indian community because we know when we connect [to] the grid outside their houses the government will listen to us, and they have listened. What we [also] did [was to go] to the substation [where] we took out the fuses [for] all these extensions. The following day they came back and reconnected us to the same grid ... because now we are touching the people that they [the ANC and government] are concerned about (T4 interview).

Edwin Futsane relates how he joined the TCC nine years ago when he was only ten and 'started learning [that] not everything is all about fighting, [there is] also legal where you can win the battle to fight the government as well. As TCC we do not just protest; we have negotiations with the government, we have engagement with them'. Such a multifaceted approach to struggle has translated into the TCC's popularity and support as Futsane, who was elected as TCC chairperson in 2017, further notes: 'You can see the difference when the ANC calls its meeting and when TCC calls its meeting, there's many; people have trust and hope in this organisation' (T5 interview). Pensioner resident Betty affirms the point: '[The] TCC has been there for the community; it's leading the community accordingly, showing the community [and] teaching the community their rights' (T2 interview).

The cumulative result is that the TCC has managed to achieve numerous successes, which by and large are hardly ever recognised by the dominant media. For Ghetto Kopane, those successes include: managing 'to bring the community together because when you are different people coming from different areas ... it's easy for you to have differences'; to get the community hooked into the electricity grid, something that 'we've [been] struggling for] for such a long time'; and to finally ensure that Thembelihle was given what is known as a 'G number' by the government, which allows for budgets to be allocated to the community (T1 interview).

In respect of the first achievement, it is crucial to note that in 2016 Thembelihle, through the TCC, was named the recipient of the Mkhaya

Migrants Award (given by the Department of Home Affairs) for the most integrated community in South Africa. However, until today the R100 000 monetary prize that goes with the award remains unpaid (T4 interview).

ROLE OF THE STATE

While there can be no denying that the ending of formal apartheid and the coming to power of a democratic government was a huge victory for the black majority in South Africa, there can also be no denying that most poor black people have remained poor since 1994. Coupled to this structural economic reality has been a continuation of class rule and politics by the democratic government – that is, poor people being treated differently, almost like second-class citizens. The TCC and many Thembelihle residents would appear to agree. In old-age pensioner Betty's words:

> Our own government take us as just ants … they don't treat us like people who are normal. This government reminds me of the apartheid government. During apartheid they – the very same people who are leading us today – used to say, here are the white people they oppress us; but today it's the same black people who oppress us … (T2 interview).

Or take the following comments from Bhayiza Miya:

> What we have picked up is that the democratically elected government was using the very same legislation of apartheid, of taking the 1913 Land Act to say poor people must be moved far away from the cities, far away from the schools and the clinics … away from … your bond houses ... it was like a class issue; 'these are people who are poor, they cannot [stay]' (T4 interview).

Miya goes on to provide a good practical example related to the community's endless but still unsuccessful attempts to get government to replace the pit latrine toilets that the community has had to use since Thembelihle became a settlement.

> We said to them let us have flushing toilets because there are sewer pipes in Thembelihle … the Indian sewer pipes [ones that service Lenasia] go through Thembelihle. When the very same sewer pipes burst, they burst inside Thembelihle; [so that] you'll find sewers running in our streets. And the very same people that are smelling this sewer … don't have flushing toilets (T4 interview).

A similar class-framed tale is related by TCC leader Siphiwe Segodi in respect of the dolomite argument made by government to justify the need to move the entire community to a safer place. The TCC 'thought, no, this was just an excuse to get us out because also obviously the Indian people … they did not want us around … they felt that Thembelihle … is resulting [in] the value of their properties declining. They put pressure on government' (T7 interview).

Even when it comes to the TCC's consistent efforts to talk to and engage with government, the feeling and experience remains one of being treated differently. 'They can't talk to us, they can't come close to us … there is always a boundary between us and them. The reason is because we are poor; it's why they always treat us like that, always fighting … shooting [as if we are] animals not people' (T3 interview).

Ghetto Kopane offers a different angle on government's behaviour, arguing that it has always wanted 'to prove this organisation called TCC wrong' and thus has consistently refused to give the TCC proper recognition and respect. He cites two examples: former Gauteng premier, Nomvula Mokonyane, who stated on her one visit to the community that 'as long as I'm alive you the people of Thembelihle you can't stay here'; and former Gauteng MEC for human settlements, Humphrey Mmemezi, who told the community that 'you don't know the struggle, we know the struggle'. As Kopane notes, both of these conscious and planned provocations only had the effect of strengthening the resolve of the community (T1 interview).

ROLE OF POLITICAL PARTIES

Like most poor communities in and around Johannesburg, local government and party politics in Thembelihle have been (since 1994), and
largely remain, dominated by the ANC. This is the case despite intensified and expanded anger and frustration across those communities over
the last decade or so in particular, directed at the ANC, its leaders and
representatives. Indeed, it is one of the main ironies of the South African
transition that the ANC continues to win the vast majority of elections
in poor communities across the country, yet at the same time ever-
increasing numbers of residents in these communities not only blame the
ANC for their problems, but simultaneously look to the ANC to address
and 'solve' those problems.

As is the case in Thembelihle, this seemingly counter-intuitive political
cycle has largely revolved around the abject failure of the ANC – through
its local councillors and domination of local government – to meet most
of the promises it has made to the residents (usually just before elections).
But instead of the anger, frustration and criticism of ever-larger numbers
of residents leading to the formation and growth of political party and
electoral alternatives and defeat of the ANC at the polls, it has led to the
growth of community organisations, protest as the main form of community political activism and, crucially, a rapid decline in the number
of people voting in elections, especially local elections (McKinley 2017).

Thembelihle is a classic case study in this regard but it is a case that
has been mostly ignored by the dominant media. This only further
contributes to a shallow and often misinformed understanding of the
ensuing conflict. In other words, the picture that is regularly painted is
one of a small minority of disgruntled community residents – through a
local community organisation such as the TCC – trying to cause trouble
for the democratically elected ANC who have majority support. Besides
the fact that overall turnout within the Johannesburg Municipality in the
last local government elections was just over 57 per cent (IEC 2016a),
the ANC's share of that vote stood at 44.5 per cent (IEC 2016b). Bottom

line: those who voted for the ANC constituted a significant minority of eligible voters and Thembelihle was no different.

While TCC leaders and activists do not cite the electoral numbers, they have their own explanation for this important sub-story, which goes some way in explaining why, despite electoral and institutional appearances to the contrary, the ANC is not at the centre of popular politics in a place like Thembelihle. Explaining why the ANC keeps winning the local ward election, Ghetto Kopane has a much more direct and practically oriented version:

> [It's] because of the propaganda … they [the ANC] will come to old people when they [are] going to get their pension there, they'll say, 'Gogo [Grandma], you know, you see this ANC is busy giving you this, this pension money. If you can vote for [another] party you have to know that this thing will be stopped immediately.' So if you are using that kind of propaganda to the older people, to the uneducated people, it's easy for you to keep on getting votes … (T1 interview).

While not empirically verifiable, such an explanation makes sense given the consistently obstructionist, opportunistic and ultimately anti-people role the ANC has played in and with Thembelihle. As Siphiwe Segodi cogently argues, 'The [local] ANC [has] basically towed the line of the ANC cabinet … the local councillor would bring what government wants and the ANC would move with that at the local level, that's how the ANC has been operating' (T7 interview). The practical application of this approach is captured well by Bhayiza Miya:

> During the protests, relocation, eviction and forced removals … the councillors of the ANC, the chief whip of the ANC, they were in the forefront of saying these people must be relocated. They wanted to build a mall [and] to have an industrial area [here but] they were waiting [for] us to be evicted or to be relocated. So after

that we resisted [but] they continued to build the mall. So for them it was the mall, it was devaluation of their houses, it was moving the poor away from where they are from and then dump them somewhere (T4 interview).

Cumulatively then, one of the foundational layers of the conflict in Thembelihle has been and remains the place and role of, as well as activities carried out by, the ANC. The linked characteristics of arrogance, of power and a lived sense of impunity have meant that the ANC's approach to the anger of and criticism from residents through community organisations, such as the TCC, has only fuelled the conflict. In the words of Ghetto Kopane: 'The ANC, it just started to see us [the TCC] as their opposition. The people who are on top for money, eating, they were ANC members, but during that time when people were fighting for this thing [electricity] they were not there, they used to just say, ah, those people, they are crazy, leave them' (T1 interview).

ROLE OF LAW ENFORCEMENT AND THE COURTS

Arguably, one of the most misrepresented aspects of conflict between the state and (poor) communities is when it comes to the role and activities of the police and the court system. There are few better examples than Thembelihle. As will become clear in the analysis of media coverage, the dominant media has manifestly and consistently failed to move beyond a narrative that mostly portrays protestors as being unreasonable and violent, while portraying the police and the courts as mostly just doing their jobs to restore 'law and order', with the occasional bad-apple cop or magistrate/judge going overboard.

It is a narrative that bears little resemblance to reality, a reality that can be located and communicated if there is a willingness to actually listen more carefully and in-depth to the practical experiences of residents themselves. The story of what happened to present-day TCC leader Bhayiza Miya at the hands of the police during and following the very first protest to oppose the attempted eviction of the community in 2002 refers:

> When the TCC was formed, I was not part of it ... I would say I was pushed to be a member of the TCC because [during] the first protest [for] stopping this eviction I was shot by the police.[3] I was a bystander [and] I could see when they started shooting people. The next day the police were here in their numbers ... they came and picked me up. I was taken to the police station [along with] 40 [others] who were locked up. [I was] in the police cell [for] about five days without appearing before the magistrate. Then I was taken to Protea court [but] I never appeared before the magistrate, I was taken back [to] the cell [and] the same captain [who] said I must be locked up said to me if we can find you with more than ten people we'll re-arrest you. That was the situation that led me to join the TCC. I grew up in a family where my father ... discouraged us to do any criminal activities. I can tell you, I was so proud to say I've never been arrested until the very same government came and arrested me ... that was my first time. Till today, I've been arrested nine times and these nine times I've never been found to be committing any crime. The security forces [have not been] oppressing the criminals but oppressing those who stand up and say no, we cannot live like this (T4 interview).

In a similar vein and over thirteen years after Miya's travails, the experience of Ghetto Kopane with the police only serves to confirm this reality:

> They [the police] target the leaders of Thembelihle Crisis Committee. We have been arrested on many, many, many occasions. They will come to our areas and break everything, you know breaking gates, breaking doors ... For example two years ago [in] 2015 that's when I was last arrested – they break my gate, and then they were about to break the door ... I said no I'm here [and] I opened and then

they said we came to arrest you. I asked them for what [and] they said because you were there at the community meeting, we found you addressing the meeting that side. I said yes, as the community member what's wrong for me to address the meeting because … I'm part of the community? They said [there was] no wrong but they [still] ended up taking me. The police are biased; they are on the side of ANC so they see us as criminals (T1 interview).

TCC leaders openly admit that their protests have, on occasion, been infiltrated by agents provocateurs and local *tsotsis* (criminals or gangsters), looking to take advantage of the chaos that often ensues when police start shooting tear gas and rubber bullets. But they are adamant, as evidence during the 2008 protests (where some participants attacked and looted foreign-owned spaza shops) confirms, that at both an individual and collective level, TCC members do not engage in criminal activities and, indeed, confront and try to stop those who do. Regardless, many end up with unwarranted criminal records that have a negative impact on their individual and family lives. Kopane shares his experience in this regard:

I ended up having a criminal record because of [when] I was arrested in 2011 [but] I never went to court. Recently when I went somewhere [for a job application] they checked and said we can't process your things because you've got a criminal case. I asked where did I commit a crime [and] they said at Lenasia because this thing says on the top Lenasia police station. So many comrades now have criminal cases … some of them they qualify to get jobs but it's very hard for them because of those kinds of actions that they don't know, they were just arrested, they never appeared at court, but they got [a] criminal record (T1 interview).

A much fuller and more accurate picture emerges when the voices and experiences of community activists and residents inform the narrative around the role and activities of the police and courts. When those who have been arrested many times have been beaten and injured, have spent days and even weeks locked up in jail cells and have been judged and convicted of crimes – most often all without actual cause, due process and just administration and representation – then there is clearly something wrong with the ways in which law enforcement and the justice system are conducting themselves. As Miya states, 'They [the political authorities] are using the police … to say we have failed, as politicians we have failed these people, so go and deal with them' (T4 interview).

Whether it is the police riding roughshod over the basic rights of freedom of expression, assembly and due process, or state prosecutors and magistrates colluding to ensure that protestors are not granted bail or that the bail granted is far too high for them to afford (T7 interview), the fact is that a large part of the relevant story is simply not being told, and thus not heard.

THE DOMINANT AND OTHER MEDIA

If there is one thing that every single interviewee completely agrees on it is that the way in which the dominant media has covered Thembelihle and its conflicts over the years has been largely presumptive, negative and disrespectful. This has been the case particularly when it comes to Thembelihle for two interlinked reasons: TCC and community residents have regularly found themselves on the streets, in protest and thus in open conflict with the state; and the destructive default view that the dominant media takes of poor communities in protest.

While the analysis of the dominant media will provide more specific examples, the views and experiences of the interviewees – most of whom have occasional but regular access to both the print and visual sides of the dominant media – certainly and consistently speak to the accompanying framing and impact. As Siphiwe Segodi reminds us, 'We [need to] under-stand and appreciate the role of the media and the impact of what the media is capable of' (T7 interview).

At the forefront is the failure of the dominant media to come into the community and actually talk to activists and residents – under normal, day-to-day circumstances – about their lives and experiences. This not only applies to an old-age pensioner like Cynthia who indicated that our interview with her was the very first time that anyone from outside the community had ever asked her about her personal life, her struggles and her feelings (T3 interview). It also applies to seasoned community activists and organisational spokespersons like Siphiwe Segodi, who categorically states, 'I can't recall someone [from the dominant media] coming to say I'm from the media and I want to get [your story]' (T7 interview). While Segodi does mention one instance where two international media outlets (BBC and CNN) came and spent a half-day in the community chatting with a few residents about the illegal reconnection of electricity prior to the start of the 2010 Soccer World Cup, the only examples given of any serious attempt to get the stories of activists or residents are those from allied civil society organisations and independent academics or researchers.

There is also unanimity in respect of how this failure has shaped coverage and the impact that it has on how people see Thembelihle as a community in general and the TCC and its activists more specifically. Ghetto Kopane relates this in the most specific and practical of ways:

> [The] media [is] not coming to us as such, but they phone us on the day of action. Maybe today we start [a] protest [and] then we [are] running away … because the police are chasing us. While you are on the way running, you hear your phone ringing then they say … can I interview you? You know we sometimes don't respond in a way that we [are] supposed to because of the situation we find ourselves in … So [the] media doesn't respect us accordingly … [they] just write what they like to write about us (T1 interview).

When Cynthia gets access to newspapers she says most of what she reads is them 'say[ing] [that] at Thembelihle they [are] just toyi-toyi[ing] [dance step at protest gatherings] for nothing ... that [the] people of this area are crazy, fighting ... all the time fighting' (T3 interview). Ghetto Kopane recalls that when he visited his parents in the North West Province his mother would say, 'I saw you last time on TV and then you were fighting for nothing', and that he would respond by saying, 'No, it is because that's how [you've] got it from the media' (T1 interview). For Bhayiza Miya, it was the specific experience he had with the nation's second-largest daily newspaper that has convinced him that the (dominant) media 'focuses on the bad side of things; they always focus on people that are violent':

> We had a picket about Marikana [and] I called the media – it was *The Star* if I'm not mistaken – to say we are having this picket can you come and cover the story? They said to me are you burning tyres, I said no. They said what are you doing? I said it's a peaceful picket [and] they never came (T4 interview).

Taken together, the picture painted is not simply one of individual journalists who just aren't doing their job or of a general lack of capacity and resources. Rather, it is a picture of constructed 'ignorance', selective choices and conscious bias. Two final examples suffice to make these points. For Siphiwe Segodi, it is because 'the story they tell is about [how] the land that [we] occupy, is dangerous etc., etc., but they wouldn't give enough time to [show how] we have consulted and this is what we have found [vis-à-vis the dolomite issue]' (T7 interview). For Bhayiza Miya, it is when, in 2016, Thembelihle (through the TCC) 'won the Mkhaya Award [for] the Most Integrated Community in South Africa [but yet] ... even the local media, your mainstream media, nobody [covered it]' (T4 interview).

WHAT THE FUTURE HOLDS

From the moment it came into existence, Thembelihle has been struggling, not just for the basics of life but also for the right to be a recognised and permanent community. At the practical heart of that struggle has been the battle over the dolomite issue – whether there is a scientifically verifiable geotechnical basis for removing the community (or large parts of it).

While the TCC has now sourced ample empirical evidence to show that there is no basis for the removal of the community, the final 'answer' is wrapped up in an ongoing geotechnical study that was eventually ordered – after much pressure and mobilisation by the TCC – to take place by the then mayor, Parks Tau, in 2015. Until today, however, the report has yet to be completed and there is little indication that it will be anytime soon (T7 interview). The importance of this for the future of Thembelihle cannot be over-estimated, as Siphiwe Segodi succinctly notes:

> The report of dolomite is going to have implications ... it will determine where things are going. If it's positive ... we are going to have to intensify the struggle to make sure we get what we've been waiting for ... But if the report says Thembelihle is so bad, it's going to create problems ... [that] will be a difficult one (T7 interview).

In the meantime, though, the component parts of Thembelihle's struggle for the basics continue and remain no less essential to realising the associated dreams and aspirations of its residents. In this sense, Cynthia's words are instructive: 'Yes, [things are] changing in Thembelihle [but only because] the people are fighting [for] all these things [that are] not here. [They are] coming but slowly' (T3 interview).

No more so than for pensioner Betty who has lived in a rickety, tin-roof shack for the entire 32 years that she has been in Thembelihle. Listening to her is a sharp reminder of why the struggles of those who live in Thembelihle are so much more than a perfunctory listing and/or recitation of housing 'challenges': 'The shack is not the place that one can stay in but we just do that because we are disadvantaged. [It is] meant for the livestock like goats, cattle; but because this government treats us as animals, here we are today just in the shacks. [Formal] housing ... gives you dignity as a person' (T2 interview).

It is also a reminder that it has been in the very acts of their decades-long struggle that the people of Thembelihle have, in personal/familial, organisational, political and practical terms, actually built a community. Simply because its residents do not yet have formal housing, do not yet have proper sanitation and do not yet have running water in their homes, does not make Thembelihle any less of a community, any less deserving of being listened to and respected.

PART 2

FROM THE OUTSIDE: DOMINANT VOICE

6

Dominant Media Telling and Elite Communication

Dale T. McKinley

> The media does not care about us, they never report
> things relevant to us and papers are only interested if
> there is bad news about us ... there's nothing in the papers
> that talks to us and about our struggle and lives. It's like we don't exist.
> — Blikkiesdorp resident[1]

These words ring loudly for poor people and the communities they live in across the width and breadth of South Africa. While they might not apply to all media, they apply to the dominant media in general. As captured in chapter 1, the dominant media is that collection of print and audio-visual media outfits (most often corporations), whether state or privately owned, that monopolise the framing of narrative within the media landscape.

In form, content and character, this dominant media is framed and moulded by a corporatised, neo-liberal market structure, which is a crucial component of South Africa's political economy. Since 1994, that structure has fuelled a commercial model of 'media transformation'. In turn, 'the political economy of South Africa's transformation has determined the political economy of the media – in the process setting limits, exerting pressures and closing off options for media transformation' (Duncan 2009: 22). Like all similarly situated dominant sectors within South Africa's capitalist political economy, the dominant media's 'attitude of unwillingness to address a lack of diversity of content … excludes deep and thorough reporting on, and engaging with, grassroots peoples, communities and their experiences' (Reid 2017b: 534).

There is little to no incentive – whether commercially, politically or programmatically – for the dominant media to either consistently and genuinely acknowledge or integrate the voices of the poor and marginalised precisely because they do not feature as substantive consumers in their profit-driven media market (Plaisance 2009). Rather, this media sees its main 'societal purpose' as being 'to inculcate and defend the economic, social and political agenda of privileged groups that dominate … society and the state' (Herman and Chomsky 1988).

Nowhere is this more applicable than in respect of the ways in which the dominant media, throughout the post-1994 democratic era, have told the stories of the majority of South Africa's population – the workers and poor. It is not that poor communities have no agency, no voice; indeed, that agency and voice is at the heart of popular and democratic struggle and contestation in contemporary South Africa.

Rather, the reality is that in the dominant media these are most often assumed, misrepresented, ignored and cumulatively moulded to fit the contours of an elitist narrative, discourse and thought; ultimately to serve, in one form or another, the political and economic interests of the elites. As a result, not only are the true stories of the struggles and accompanying experiences of poor communities rarely heard and/or seen as they are waged and lived, but society's overall understanding, view and approach to those struggles and experiences, and thus also to poor people themselves, is reshaped accordingly.

WHOSE VOICE, WHAT STORY?

In the earlier chapters it is the community residents whose voice(s) are central. They are the ones telling their own personal and collective stories, sharing their histories and struggles and expressing their feelings and experiences. By listening to, recording and then compiling those voices into an accumulated narrative, the story that emerges, even though it can never hope to 'tell' everything, is one that is of and belongs to the people themselves.

This section provides a cross-section analysis, covering all three communities in this book, of examples taken from a comprehensive post-1994 sampling of print articles and audio-visual clips from numerous media outlets that constitute the dominant media in South Africa. The sampling selection was determined by the audience-centred approach and a reasonably representative sample of dominant news media material. Following the audience-centred approach, we primarily considered news outlets to which a large number of South African news consumers had reasonable to high levels of access (Duncan and Reid 2013).

With regard to television broadcasting, news reports were sampled from the South African Broadcasting Corporation (SABC), eNCA and eTV. The SABC and eTV television news broadcasters were specifically selected because they are free-to-air (non-subscription) and as such hold the highest portion of television news audience share in South Africa. While the SABC is a public service broadcaster and eTV is privately owned, the ownership structures of these two broadcasters were not a determining factor in their selection.

Viewed according to an audience-centred approach, the inclusion of the SABC and eTV is important simply because more people have access to these two television news broadcasters than any other television news channel. The 24-hour news channel eNCA is carried on the subscription satellite service DSTV and is therefore only accessible to a much smaller audience segment (those with enough expendable income to afford a subscription service), but was included in the sample to gain a cross-section between free-to-air and subscription service television.

Mainstream newspapers and online print media sampled included Media24 publications (*City Press, The Witness, Daily Sun, Sunday Sun, Beeld, Die Burger, Rapport, Die Son* and the online news platform, News24. com), Independent Media (*Cape Argus, Cape Times, The Mercury, The Star, Pretoria News, Daily News, Isolezwe, Sunday Independent, Sunday Tribune* and the online news platform www.iol.co.za), Times Media/Tiso Blackstar Group (*Sunday Times, The Times, Daily Dispatch, Business Day, Sowetan, Weekend Post, The Herald* and *Sunday World*), Caxton (*The Citizen*) and Primedia (Eyewitness News – #EWN). Four independent publications were included in the sample (*Mail & Guardian, Daily Maverick, Daily Vox* and *GroundUp*) in order to perform a comparison between independent and mainstream news media outlets. Some of the titles and outlets listed here did not contain any coverage of any of the three communities and were therefore not included in the media content analysis. Therefore, while we aimed to produce a sample of 140 articles/ broadcasts per community, this was only achieved for Glebelands. For Thembelihle, we drew a sample of 127, and for Xolobeni/Amadiba, 122. A total of 389 news reports were analysed.

Included in the sampling is a section linked to 'independent publications'. These do not include community media outfits but are either small-scale private (for-profit) units (for example, *Daily Maverick*), or civil society, non-profit media organisations (for example, *GroundUp*). All of them are online entities and they have been included not because of their ownership structures or their accessibility to the audience, but rather because of their regular impact on agenda-setting in the dominant media. In South Africa, news stories are regularly initiated by independent publications, and are subsequently picked up and reported on further by mainstream news media outlets. The decision to include a sample of independent publications was also informed by historical media events, most especially the 2012 news coverage of the Marikana massacre, as discussed in chapter 1. In that instance, it was independent publications that first reported the scale and true character of the killings, while the mainstream media initially and unquestioningly represented the version of events as narrated by officialdom until such time as this version was exposed as a non-truth.

We did not include community media outlets in our sample. This was a considered decision informed by various factors. Firstly, for the most part, the community media in South Africa do not form part of the dominant media. Where the dominant media is comprised of a collection of media outlets that generally and collectively contribute to sculpting the character and trajectory of the narrative on any particular event or story, it is exceedingly rare for a community media outlet to have a noteworthy influence on the shaping of a story in the national discourse. Of course, there are exceptions, but these are few. Secondly, from an audience-centred perspective and with a view to the media repertoires or news appetites of the majority of mass communications users in South Africa, the community media show remarkably low levels of access (Angelopulo and Potgieter 2020). Thirdly, we recognise that community media outlets often tell stories and represent voice(s) differently to the dominant media, which is exceedingly valuable, but that was not the focus or the scope of this study. The aim of this research was to offer an analysis of the difference between stories as told by grassroots voice(s) and the manner in which the same events are represented by the dominant media, recognising that it is the dominant media that plays a principal role in shaping the national discourse.

The main purpose of the analysis below is twofold: to reveal key differences, contradictions, omissions and indeed completely opposite 'tellings' between the stories told by the residents and those contained in the dominant media, and to subject the storytelling of the dominant media to both objective and subjective critique.

Each news article and report was individually assessed to determine the sources of information that were used to produce the story. Sources were included in the coding where a news report clearly identified that a person (whether their name was provided or only their affiliation or position) had contributed to the information presented in the news report, and/or persons with whom the journalist had consulted directly. At times sources were quoted verbatim in news reports, and in other instances they were paraphrased: both instances were counted as sources on the grounds that the news report bore evidence of having being informed by a particular source. In a small number of cases, it was not possible to determine the source of information used to produce the news report. Sources were then coded only in cases where the information was clearly attributed to a particular source.

Each time a source was identified in a news report, the source was allocated and counted according to a particular category as indicated in the figures below. In some cases, multiple sources belonging to the same category appeared in the same news report (for example, sometimes two or three members of the South African Police Service (SAPS) were used as sources for the same news report). Initially, these sources were counted and recorded separately. Thereafter, categories were collated to reflect the number of times news articles had acquired information from a particular source category. So, for example, we assessed the number of times news articles relied on information from the police, or the number of times news articles relied on information from government officials, or from the business/private sector, or from community members and so on. In this way, we were able to assess the degree to which journalists relied on each particular source category to inform their reporting.

Adopting this method of coding was also important with regard to the validity of the findings. In some cases, a news report consulted multiple sources from one category. For example, two news reports each cited five separate sources from the category of community members (Nkosi 2013; Phala 2016). Had these sources been counted individually they would have been averaged across the entire sample, thus skewing the results. In other words, the numbers would have shown that community members were consulted by journalists on ten occasions, when in actual fact this work was done by only two journalists on two occasions. It was important then to ascertain how often each separate news report (and

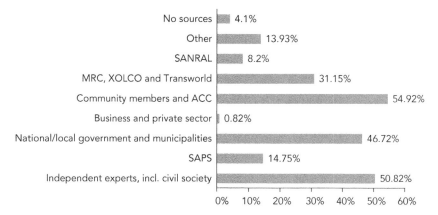

Figure 6.1: Xolobeni/Amadiba: total percentages of sources in news reports

each journalist) relied on each separate source category, rather than individual sources from each category, to make the news.

With regard to the sources used to generate news stories, the breakdown for the three communities are as illustrated below.

Community members and/or representatives of the Amadiba Crisis Committee (ACC) were consulted by journalists in 54.92 per cent of news reports. As Figure 6.1 indicates, this category of sources was cited more frequently than any other. However, this is not necessarily an indication that the voice(s) of the community members are featured with much prominence. Firstly, the higher percentage score for this category is largely due to the fact that the ACC has appointed an extremely active spokesperson, Nonhle Mbuthuma. In the largest majority of news reports where a community member from Xolobeni/Amadiba is cited by a journalist, that community member is Nonhle. Were it not for Nonhle's diligent engagement with the media, there would be very few community voices in news reports.

When we visited Nonhle she told us that almost all of the interaction she has with journalists is conducted telephonically when journalists call her to ask for her comment. This indicates a sparse presence of journalistic activity in the region, where journalists seldom travel to Amadiba to perform basic investigative work, such as collecting a variety of first-hand accounts from assorted sources, or engaging meaningfully with the persons most directly

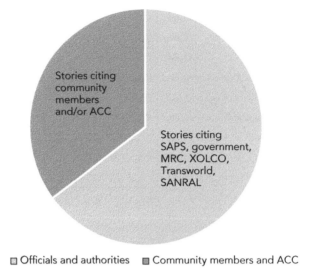

Officials and authorities ▣ Community members and ACC

Figure 6.2: Xolobeni/Amadiba: community sources versus officials and authorities

impacted by events by conducting in-depth interviews in order to under-stand the history and context of a story. For most journalists, capturing a few-second telephonic sound bite from Nonhle is enough.

Secondly, while 54.92 per cent of news reports may contain a refer-ence to a community member (most often Nonhle), this pales to a much smaller portion of the overall representation of voice(s) when the sources of 'officialdom' are not separated, as we have done in Figure 6.1, but are rather seen collectively.

While news reports on Xolobeni/Amadiba contained references to community members as sources a total of 67 times, sources from the SAPS, national/provincial government or municipalities, Mineral Resource Commodities (MRC), Xolobeni Empowerment Company (XOLCO), Transworld Energy and Minerals and/or the South African National Roads Agency (SANRAL) were used 123 times. The voice(s) of the community are therefore heavily outweighed by the voice(s) of officials and authorities. This trend is even more prevalent when assessing the news coverage of Glebelands, with respect to community voice(s).

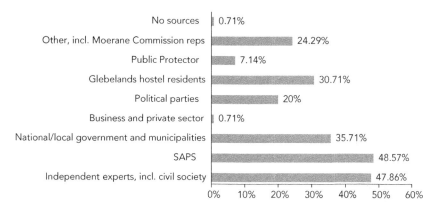

Figure 6.3: Glebelands: total percentages of sources in news reports

Only 30.71 per cent of news reports on Glebelands contained evidence of journalists sourcing information from one or more Glebelands hostel resident/s. Moreover, where a Glebelands hostel resident was cited as a source in a news report, this was most often because the resident was quoted while giving testimony before the Moerane Commission. There is extremely scarce evidence of journalists visiting the Glebelands hostel area or actively seeking the voice(s) of community residents.

As illustrated in Figure 6.4, reports cited Glebelands hostel residents as sources (mostly Moerane Commission testimony) 43 times, while news stories cited the SAPS, national/provincial government or municipalities, political parties or the Public Protector as sources 156 times. Once again, the voice(s) of community members are heavily outweighed by the voices of officials and authorities. In this respect, the extent to which the Moerane Commission boosted the news reporting of conditions in Glebelands and the representation of community voice(s) can itself be read as evidence of an elite bias on the part of the dominant media. The tragic story of the assassinations and violence taking place at Glebelands were not enough on their own to draw the gaze of the dominant media. Instead, an official commission (an elite exercise) was required to gain news media attention.

There is a point to be made about journalists being unwilling or unable to visit the localities of Glebelands and Amadiba. The Glebelands hostel complex has been the site of continuous violence and murders for a long time. While this did not deter us from conducting our own interviews with hostel residents in Glebelands, it is understandable that some journalists might be fearful to enter the area. Xolobeni is a particularly remote region, access to which requires a pretty adventurous (though not impossible) 4×4 vehicle journey over some tough terrain. Financial constraints experienced by newsrooms may prevent journalists from making the trip from their desks to the remote red sand dunes of Amadiba.

However, in Thembelihle, none of these aspects are at play. Thembelihle is easy to access: literally anyone can walk straight into the settlement from one of the arterial roads that border the community. It is also situated a short distance from the centre of Johannesburg, where most of South Africa's dominant media outlets either have their main office or at least a satellite office. Yet, our findings reveal that the dominant media's treatment of voice(s) in its reporting on the community of Thembelihle followed the same trends as for Glebelands and Xolobeni. While fearfulness with regard to personal safety and financial constraints may certainly

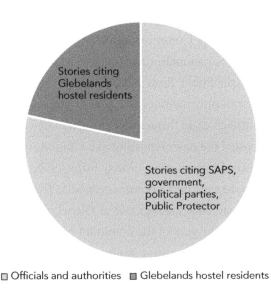

Stories citing Glebelands hostel residents

Stories citing SAPS, government, political parties, Public Protector

□ Officials and authorities ■ Glebelands hostel residents

Figure 6.4: Glebelands: community sources versus officials and authorities

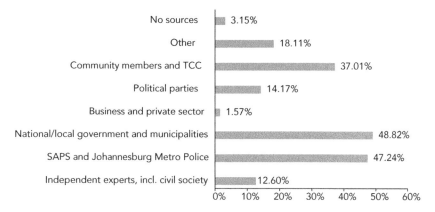

Figure 6.5:   Thembelihle: total percentages of sources in news reports

negatively impact news gathering, these cannot be the sole determining factors for explaining the dominant media's lack of representation of community and grassroots voice(s).

Regarding the news reports on Thembelihle, 37.01 per cent of news stories used community residents or representatives of the Thembelihle Crisis Committee (TCC) as sources of information. The largest majority of these community sources were protestors on occasions when the Thembelihle community initiated protests over either the lack of basic services to their community or against the ever-present threat of eviction. Again, this revealed a lack of evidence to suggest engaged journalistic activity in the area. Journalists appear to talk to Thembelihle residents only at protests, but do not actively seek out community voice(s) when compiling stories to a more meaningful degree, and do not conduct in-depth interviews with those at the centre of the story.

Thembelihle community members or the TCC were cited as sources in news reports 47 times, while the SAPS, national/provincial government or municipalities and political parties were used as sources 140 times, and again the voices of officials and authorities dominated the news reportage when compared to community members' voice(s).

Our initial source analysis was followed by a more in-depth narrative analysis, which compares and contrasts the nature and character of

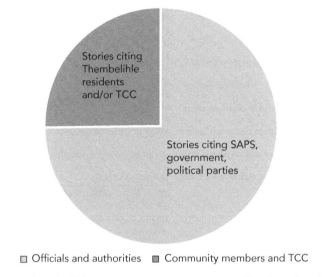

Stories citing Thembelihle residents and/or TCC

Stories citing SAPS, government, political parties

☐ Officials and authorities ■ Community members and TCC

Figure 6.6:   Thembelihle: community sources versus officials and authorities

storytelling and framing performed by the media with the stories related to us by the community members themselves. This analysis follows in the sections below.

GLEBELANDS

One of the most notable and instructive general trends to surface from the sampling is that for the dominant media the Glebelands story hardly constituted a blip on their radar screen until lots of blood started to flow. Of the 115 sample articles and clips accessed, less than 10 per cent are from before 2014 when the murder count was just beginning to rise. The vast majority of those before then – and there are not many – only mention Glebelands in passing as part of a much broader focus on hostel-related conflict between the African National Congress (ANC) and Inkatha Freedom Party (IFP) from the mid- to late 1990s.

With specific reference to the print media, there is very little coverage during 2013–2014 when the violence began to take a firmer grip. More specifically, one of the country's largest media conglomerates,

Independent Media, had absolutely no coverage during 2014–2015. Private television outfit eNCA/eTV had no clips for 2015 and only one for the entirety of 2017.

Moreover, a sizeable majority of the print and audio-visual coverage is concentrated on the Moerane Commission hearings, which focused on political killings in KwaZulu-Natal Province and which ran from late 2016 to early 2018. Besides confirming the extremely limited attention span of the dominant media, what is crucial to note here is that the only reason some of the more detailed and first-hand stories told by residents and their activist supporters made their way into the pages and onto the screens was because of the testimony they gave at the Moerane Commission. Prior to the Commission, there was hardly any reporting of these stories, and where aspects of them were covered, they were constantly questioned and/or presented as suspect.

Another general trend is the varying figures given for the number of people killed at Glebelands. For example, a *TimesLive* article in July 2017 stated that the number of killings at that time was 89; and, yet, at the same time, a *News24* article claimed that the number was 93. Glebelands residents and activists who have monitored and recorded the killings closely, some of whom were interviewed by us, attest that the number of deaths in July 2017 was already well over 100. What this reveals is lazy journalism, a 'we don't really care' attitude, combined with a not so thinly disguised classism. This is something that would never be accepted if those who were being killed were wealthy residents of upmarket urban areas, such as Johannesburg's Sandton or Cape Town's Constantia.

Yet a further trend that points to a lack of empirical or contextual depth is the complete absence of any follow-up on and/or critical interrogation of what is being reported and claimed. A pertinent example is the numerous articles and clips that meticulously list all the security-related measures that have been taken at Glebelands (for example, CCTV cameras, fencing, police and private security patrols), presenting them as evidence of how the authorities are concretely and proactively addressing the murders. But that is where things end, with no subsequent reporting, inclusive of numerous residents' voices, on whether such measures have actually had any meaningful impact and effectiveness or whether they have even been functionally maintained.

As explained in chapter 3, when we interviewed the Glebelands residents they expressed disdain for these 'security measures', maintaining that they had done nothing to stem the tide of violence and killings, were entirely ineffective and were put in place without any consultation with the residents themselves. Interviewees mentioned, for example, how murders had occurred within view of the CCTV cameras but that the footage had never been used to arrest or charge the killers. Nonetheless, the dominant media's repeated mention of the security-related measures continually framed the narrative as one in which the authorities were seen to be doing something effective to alleviate the violence, when in reality these measures proved useless. Solid follow-up investigative reporting ought to have exposed this reality, but it did not.

Likewise, there is little critical interrogation in respect of the claims and promises made by police, politicians and government officials. For example, an SABC clip from 13 May 2016 is largely filled by a monologue (masquerading as an interview) from a SAPS brigadier who makes all sorts of claims that the police are not only doing a great job containing the violence but are warmly welcomed by Glebelands residents. Not only does the journalist fail to ask any serious questions, she openly accepts everything the brigadier says. In general, across all media platforms, police, government officials and politicians are treated as if their rank or position confers absolute trust in their word.

In another example, a 19 October 2016 *Cape Argus* article makes extensive mention of important remedial actions proposed in the Public Protector's report on Glebelands, actions supported by the vast majority of Glebelands residents. Ever since though, there has been a deafening silence in that paper and all others, a silence that treats those proposed actions as if they were meaningless, as if it makes no difference to the thousands of people whether they are implemented or not. For the dominant media, it appears this is just another in a long list of tick-the-boxes reporting when it comes to the lives of the poor, the forgotten.

In a similar vein, a 10 May 2016 article in *The Herald* covered (along with other media outlets) the arrest of a Glebelands hit man. This was a significant event, given that it marked the first time that any of the by now well-known and high-profile killers of Glebelands residents had been apprehended and charged. Regardless, there has hardly been a mention of what has since happened to this case. Instead, the dominant media simply jumps to the next killing or next arrest and conducts no inquiry, even briefly, into whether anyone is actually being held responsible. The result is that the story remains largely untold, in respect of the perpetrator(s), the victims and those supposedly duty-bound to serve and protect.

When it comes to the ways in which the dominant media frames and 'explains' the conflict and violence at Glebelands, it is clear that they have largely chosen to ignore and/or dismiss the voices and views of the residents themselves and of their activist and civil society supporters. Rather, it is the views and opinions of state officialdom, of those associated with the ruling party, which are privileged and often simply parroted.

There are numerous examples of this. In an SABC clip from 30 December 2015, which is dominated by interviews with the police, municipal officials and senior provincial politicians including the then provincial premier, the journalist accepts and then repeats, as fact, their recurring claim that it is the 'allocation of rooms' that is the 'root cause' of the conflict and violence. And again, in two clips from eNCA on 24 August and 25 September 2014, both of which have no resident voice(s) and provide no history or context, the violence is ascribed to 'unelected block chairmen' who are 'selling rooms' in the first clip, while the second one puts it down to petty factionalism and 'leadership squabbles over the last 20 years'. Compare this to the actual voices of the interviewees who repeatedly state that the root causes of the violence and conflict are corrupt politicians, government officialdom and the police.

What this highlights, yet again, is how most journalists simply accept the picture provided by the voices of officialdom, of the powerful and connected, without engaging with the very people who are actually living in and through the story.

The dominant media's construction of a mostly decontextualised, ahistorical, classist, secondary-source centred and elite-framed narrative is exposed even more when compared to the samplings from independent publications. Take a *Mail & Guardian* piece from 24 July 1998, which stands apart in providing meaningful historical gravitas and context to the violence and killings, a full 15 years before the present scourge began. Or another article from the same publication on 14 June 2015, which is the only one to actually detail the role of Glebelands hit man kingpin, Bongani Hlope, and his alleged connections with local police and high-ranking ANC politicians in the province, as well as pointing out how so many of the witness accounts made by residents to the police are lost or simply ignored.

Then there is the *GroundUp* article from 28 November 2014, which, instead of parroting the police and politicians, actually engages in some investigative and research work to shed light on the complex, organic history of block committees. In doing so, it reveals how, when a majority of those committees began to actively oppose undemocratic directives coming from the politically connected ANC councillor and his supporters, they were 'dissolved' by the then provincial premier, Senzo Mchunu.

It is the small and underfunded *GroundUp* that then does what none of the dominant media outlets, with their national/regional reach and sizeable budgets, have managed to do. In a piece from 13 March 2015, one of the central and most controversial figures in the Glebelands story, the local ANC councillor Robert Mzobe, is tracked down and interviewed. Not only does the interview expose the dominant media's failure to undertake basic journalistic tasks (something akin to not interviewing former president Jacob Zuma about the Nkandla scandal), it allows the readers to see for themselves what kind of person Mzobe is and what he actually thinks of the residents' lives lost in his political constituency. In Mzobe's words: 'I'm not going to defend myself about something that is not true … There are so many people dying in KwaZulu-Natal every day; Glebelands is not the only place that experiences death.'

XOLOBENI/AMADIBA

Similar to the Glebelands sampling, the coverage of Xolobeni/Amadiba by the dominant media is principally defined by a historically and analytically shallow and reactive approach. This helps explain its time- and content-bound character, in which a small minority of articles and clips spread out over a 20-year period deal with the N2 toll road issue, while a large majority of samples focus on the mining struggle but only start in 2015.

Other than confirming the absence of any consistent or meaningful coverage, especially in relation to the mining, prior to the onset of sustained outside interest (for example, through legal cases, the release of a documentary film,[2] and increased government events/presence in the area), this overall frame reveals two crucial things: the general marginalisation of those communities and areas that are not urban/peri-urban – noting that most of the coverage of the N2 toll road issue comes from local/regional papers in the Media24 stable; and the largely reactive timelines and decontextualised attention spans of the dominant media centred on dramatic acts of violence (in this case, the mafia-like murder of ACC chairperson Sikhosiphi 'Bazooka' Radebe in early 2016).

The sampling gives specific concrete empirical evidence to the above. There is no better example than the fact that for the SABC only eight clips could be located over the last 22 years. Not only are all of them concentrated in a three-year span, from 2015–2017, but just three focus on the mining issue and all of these are within a two-month period from March to April 2016.

For South Africa's main private news television channel, eNCA/eTV, no coverage was found prior to 2015. While things are marginally better in terms of the quantity of coverage on the print media side, that does not apply to Primedia, which carried only five articles, all of which focus on the murder of Bazooka Radebe.

Also similar to the Glebelands media sampling is the practice of regularly presenting the opinions and claims of various representatives of officialdom. Such practice is directly linked to the just as regular absence or general sidelining of resident and community voice(s).

Every clip from the SABC on the N2 toll road sounds like a government propaganda piece, most notably because hardly anything or anyone in opposition makes the cut. In a feature carried on 31 August 2008 in the *Sunday Independent* (which at the time was an influential and widely read national Sunday paper), the entire mining conflict is presented through the views of government spokespersons and contains not a single resident/community voice.

Further, in many of the clips and articles, the issue of job creation (whether in relation to the mining or the N2 projects) is talked about repeatedly by those in support of the mine, ranging from the MRC and its black economic empowerment subsidiaries, to government, to some traditional authorities. Specifically, a 15 April 2016 *Independent Online* piece includes exaggerated claims by MRC-affiliated individuals of the job creation that would flow from the mine's establishment, as well as claims that the mine's 'public participation processes' are being hampered by violence perpetrated by the ACC. These stand as unquestioned 'fact'. What makes the ways in which particular claims about job creation so crucial is that they are at the epicentre of the whole 'development of the community' argument, which posits that the introduction of mining will always and consistently bring positive socio-economic 'development' to the community.

It thus appears to make no difference to the dominant media that the actual community has much to say about the kind of 'development' and thus jobs they desire. When we interviewed community members, they were cognisant of the need to encourage development in their home region, but insisted that they ought to be allowed to select for themselves what type of development that should be. Many of them favoured, for example, the expansion of ecotourism in the area as opposed to the mining project and the upgrading of the existing road network as opposed to the brand new and singular N2 highway.

Arguably two of the most egregious elements that emerge from the sampling (the conscious yet subtle ways in which the whole conflict is presented as an internal community matter, and the casting of those against the N2 and mining projects as a minority of malcontents and even criminals) is included without any questioning or critical interrogation. The best example of the former is an eNCA/eTV clip from 28 March 2016, which begins with this gem: 'The government has sent a team to try to reduce tensions in an area where people are divided.' Just like that, the entire conflict is reduced to a fight among 'people' in the 'area', in which, of course, the government is playing a mediating role. The rest of the story that follows is framed by this initial lie.

The best examples of the latter are two articles in the *City Press* (11 May and 7 September 2008). In the first piece, the local chief, who energetically endorses the mining project and labels those against it as a small minority, is uncritically presented as speaking on behalf of the entire 'community'. This despite the fact that the very same community had already exposed the chief as being part of the pro-mining set-up and selling them out for the price of a 4×4 vehicle and a XOLCO directorship. In the second piece, the chairperson of XOLCO is quoted, again without any questioning, as claiming that the violence can be ascribed to 'criminal' elements in the community, has nothing to do with the mining and that only a small minority of people oppose the mine. Our own investigations and interviews reveal that this is untrue. Had the *City Press* journalists engaged in any meaningful way with the very people who stand to be most directly affected by the mine, they would have heard a different side of the story.

There is also the matter of articles and clips produced within the same media outlet being completely disconnected from each other. In other words, there is no content consistency across the various pieces of coverage, which, in turn, translates into a serious deficit of institutional/journalistic memory. Take the community's ecotourism initiative as an example: a thriving project in its early phases, the demise of which opened up a pathway for both the mining project and the N2 toll road to become the substitute 'pathway to development'.

An *Independent Online* article from 15 April 2016, while revealing that Zamile Qunya is the founder of XOLCO, says nothing about either when he took up this position or what he was doing beforehand. And yet articles in the same stable of papers from years back profiled Qunya as a community resident and leader in charge of running the ecotourism project. As a result of the failure to connect their own dots, readers have no idea of Qunya's history, no reference points for why he would shift from the ecotourism project to becoming the main 'community' champion and beneficiary of a contra-mining project.

Similarly, a 15 November 2006 article in *The Herald* (owned by the Times Media/Tiso Blackstar group) revealed that in 2002 the ecotourism project was named as one of the most 'outstanding community tourism enterprises' by then president Thabo Mbeki, as part of his annual Presidential Awards. Yet, there has been no further mention of this hugely important part of the history of the Xolobeni/Amadiba story in any of the group's titles. It has been airbrushed from the story and so too has a fuller and truthful understanding of that history.

There are a few rare examples of journalists within the dominant media who have managed to provide exceptions to the rule. The investigative news programme *CheckPoint*, part of the eNCA/eTV outfit, ran a three-part 'Murderous Mines' series in 2016, which although centred on the murder of Bazooka Radebe, provided in-depth historical background to MRC's involvement and gave ample space for various community voice(s). An article in the *Sunday Tribune* from 1 July 2007 shows what time well spent and a basic commitment to privileging the voice(s) of the affected community can produce. This is achieved through actually being in the community, attending a local meeting and spending time talking with a variety of residents. The result is a piece that is true to a principled journalistic purpose – to tell a story by listening to those who are its main characters.

Again, though, it is among the independent publications that one sees the extent to which the dominant media has been and remains such substandard storytellers when it comes to poor rural communities like Xolobeni/Amadiba. The way in which a *GroundUp* article from 6 November 2015 does this is simple: it digs deep enough to find a '2014 report by the Eastern Cape Department of Economic Development which found that surrounding communities were unanimous in their opposition to the mine as it would destroy their livelihoods and the environment and ruin any prospect of ecotourism in the area'. And, just like that, not only does the article put paid to the repeated claims of equivalency between pro- and anti-mining groups within the community, but the untruths of the MRC and its allies are exposed for untruths.

Almost standing alone is Stephan Hofstatter's *Mail & Guardian* piece from 4 May 2007, which takes multiple interviews conducted with pro-mining individuals and then subjects the associated claims to critical interrogation informed and buttressed by the voices of numerous community residents. By doing so, Hofstatter does not become the main narrator himself; he becomes the vessel for allowing the voices that count to both frame and tell the story.

THEMBELIHLE

Combined with the fact that Thembelihle is located in the country's largest and wealthiest metropolis, which is also home to the headquarters of both the public broadcaster (SABC) as well as most of South Africa's dominant media houses, the concomitant expectation would be that there would be no shortage of coverage of its struggles.

While the copy count of the dominant print media has been quite substantial (despite being mostly shallow), the same is not the case for television. Only nine clips in total could be found for the SABC. This is astonishing given the SABC's public broadcaster mandate, the proximity of Thembelihle as well as the extended timeframe of its struggles and the sheer number of protests or events. When it comes to eNCA/eTV, all ten of the clips located were from a three-month period (February to April) in 2015. Suffice to say that these kinds of figures and timeframe spread of coverage are a separate story in itself.

The almost complete absence of coverage by the dominant media of arguably the most intense and sustained period of conflict and violence during the 2001/2002 struggle over the attempted forced removal of the entire community bears witness to this.

Two pieces carried by *The Star* (part of the Independent Media stable) on 12 April 1999 and 7 November 2002 are typical examples of how articles in the same paper dealing with same issue – in this case the dolomite problem – can be so disconnected as to completely contradict each other. While the first article points out that the government lacks empirical proof for their argument that because all of Thembelihle is located on dolomitic land the community needs to be moved, the second article simply parrots the government's argument that the whole area is 'unfit for human habitation'.

In a similar vein, a 15 May 2015 piece carried on Primedia's EWN features the announcement that the government has finally declared Thembelihle as a 'housing project', thus opening the door to official budgets being allocated for selected 'development' initiatives. Regardless of the fact that this represents a huge victory for the community, and confirms that after 20 years of obfuscation, the government has finally faced the nonsensical reality of its dolomite argument, not one further article or clip could be found that includes or uses this crucial development. Instead, the dominant media simply keeps repeating government's dolomite arguments.

In a *Sunday Times* article on 11 September 1994, Dan Bovu, later to become the long-serving but widely despised ANC councillor for Thembelihle, is interviewed as the chairperson of the Thembelihle 'residents' association'. Bovu proceeds to talk about how the community has been struggling to get government to provide housing subsidies and to develop the area, and expresses his suspicion that the government geological survey on dolomite is not accurate and is being used as a cover to remove the community.

Alarmingly, in the ensuing 23 years, and more especially during the many years that Bovu was councillor and at the centre of the conflict with residents over precisely the same issues, not once is any of this mentioned in any of the articles coming out of the Times Media/Tiso Blackstar group or any of the other publications of the dominant print media. This reveals two crucial things: that despite the core issues having remained the same for over 23 years, the dominant media has engaged in a self-constructed exercise of mass amnesia; and this has led to the complete atomisation of Thembelihle's story wherein the means to make logical and interpretive sense of its history have been conveniently removed.

In contradistinction, there are a few rare examples of the kind of journalism that can be produced when sufficient history and context is provided to produce a fuller and more truthful story. Take, for instance, Maureen Isaacson's 11 September 2011 article in the *Sunday Independent*, which provides a substantive explanatory background to many of the causes behind Thembelihle's long-running conflict, including the role of the councillors and the corruption behind the failure of even basic development projects. She is able to write such a piece because she did her research and spent time talking and listening to community residents. Then there is the *Daily Vox* (an independent publication) piece from 5 July 2016, which concentrates its focus on (parts of) Thembelihle finally getting electricity. Here is a well-researched, well-presented and informative article, which lays out the story, from the perspective and experience of residents, of the struggle for electricity ever since Thembelihle became a community.

Similar to the experience that other poor communities have had with the dominant media, the coverage of Thembelihle is filled with negative and pejorative characterisations of residents and activists. This even goes to the extent of calling people, who at the time the *Sowetan* article was written on 22 January 2003 had been on the land and established a community for almost 20 years, 'squatters'. This is the direct result of not taking the time to talk and listen, of not making a human connection and of being able to see people as much more than the opportunistic land invader, the angry face, the troublesome complainer and the violent protestor that they are most often assumed and described as being. Two specific examples make the broadly applicable point.

A clip from the SABC on 23 February 2015 gives itself away by its very title – 'Thembelihle informal settlement residents on a violent service delivery protest'. True to titular form, the clip proceeds to confirm its own preframed judgement by describing the residents as 'violent' without providing anything other than shots of a few burning tyres and other objects being placed across a road. Nothing is said or shown about the reasons the residents felt it necessary to block the road, the actions of either the residents or the police prior to the road scenes or the actions of the police in 'dispersing' the protestors. The residents are thus presented and seen as silent figures, with no agency other than to toyi-toyi, shout and run.

A Media24 article from 16 September 2011 gives 100 per cent voice to government; everything that those voices say is presented as fact with no critical interrogation. And here's what they say: the entire area is dolomitic and thus the people must leave, the community is 'violent' and their leaders are 'hooligans'. There is no mention of the previous attempts to forcibly relocate the community, no mention of the counter-reports on the dolomite, no mention of the dire basic services situation and no mention of any of the innumerable attempts by the community to engage the authorities through official channels.

In the dominant media there is virtually no positive news or reporting about poor communities in conflict. The prime example is the virtual silence around what happened during the xenophobic violence in 2008, which saw the outbreak of both organised and indiscriminate or opportunistic attacks by South Africans against (largely African) immigrants, most of which took place in poor communities in the provinces of Gauteng and KwaZulu-Natal. As detailed in chapter 5, the TCC successfully mobilised residents to embrace and celebrate the community's immigrant residents, going so far as to track down and return goods stolen from immigrant spaza shops. Additionally, the dominant media had hardly anything to say during the ensuing years as this humanity and nationalist-free community spirit took such a hold in Thembelihle that in 2016 it was given the Mkhaya Migrants Award by the Department of Home Affairs for the most integrated community in South Africa. Yet again, it has been left to independent publications, exemplified by an article in the *Daily Vox* on 19 May 2015, to share the positive side of things; in this case, by allowing residents to express the lived inclusivity of their community.

As has been shown in the two other community case studies, when it comes to Thembelihle there is also a broad failure of the dominant media to critically question and engage police action in general, and, more specifically, what happens after people get arrested. These include, for example, basic violations of the protest rights of residents and enforcement of the relevant laws; shootings, which are often without warning; pre-emptive surveillance and intimidation; beatings and torture in police cells; and violations of laws in respect of due process, incarceration without charge and bail hearings.

Rather, what is reported is that residents engaged in a violent protest, police responded accordingly and some people were arrested and charged (almost always for public violence and/or destruction of property). When it comes to post-arrest realities, there might be the rare reporting of a conviction or acquittal. But, there is nothing about the documented abuse of the prosecutorial system to victimise and punish legitimate protest and activism as was the case when Ghetto Kopane was convicted of a crime without any proper court appearance and without ever being notified.

Such is also the case with an eNCA/eTV piece on 19 March 2015 covering the upcoming court appearance of 32 Thembelihle residents on charges of public violence. That was the end of the story; there was no further coverage of how long the trial went on (as it happened, for months due to endless postponements requested to allow the police more time to make their case) or whether any/some/all of the accused were convicted (as it turned out all charges were dropped).

There is one final but very crucial aspect of what lies behind the character of the dominant media's coverage of a poor community in conflict, such as Thembelihle. It is the almost complete lack of any basic research and/or effort to reach out to relevant community organisations (in this case, the TCC) to source materials and documents that provide a history of their struggle. If any had done so, as we did, they would have found a paper trail of numerous memorandums, letters, reports, minutes of meetings and, yes, even some media articles. Without these, it is impossible to tell the full story, not only in respect of the efforts and activities of the community and its organisations to use the democratic and institutional space (that is, to follow the 'rules') but in respect of placing the responses and subsequent actions of the state in proper context (that is, who is being unreasonable, who is not following the rules and who is interested in finding real solutions).

Applying the above to the issue of dolomitic ground, almost every article and clip produced by the dominant media has accepted, at face value, the government's claims that the area is unsafe for human habitation and thus for further development. Yet, there are official documents and reports available in the TCC archive that provide ample evidence that the government's claims are not what they appear to be. Specifically, there is the 2004 report on dolomite risk conducted under the auspices of Webber Wentzel Bowens law firm on behalf of the TCC and the minutes of a City of Johannesburg technical team meeting in 2007 showing a city council resolution in 2005 agreeing to develop part of Thembelihle, as well as an admittance that the city lacks sufficient information on the dolomite issue.

There is a strong case to be made that the vast majority of the dominant media has not simply failed to carry out basic journalistic tasks but has engaged in an elitist and classist narrative and continues to do so. It begs the question: what do you think would happen if the City of Johannesburg insisted on forcibly moving a significant section of the Morningside suburb in Sandton, citing dolomite as the main grounds? The dominant media would be all over it and would make sure they had every single study and expert opinion in hand: the double standards are deafening.

CONSTRUCTION AND DISSEMINATION

The dominant media in South Africa largely reflects the views and interests of those who possess dominant political, economic, social and cultural power, as well as position. The practical result in most cases is that the content and choices of the stories that the dominant media tells replicate and reinforce the parallel and dominant discourses and thought in South African society; that is, a separate but linked and mutually reinforcing construction. This is then extended beyond the reach of the dominant media by the consequent dissemination and reproduction of the storylines through a range of elite channels of communication, both public and private. In metaphorical terms, the small top part of the societal pyramid casts its elitist shadow across the much larger bottom base and, in the process, constantly reshapes and moulds society's view of the pyramid itself.

There are two useful examples of the construction 'set', both of which are representative of significant aspects of the community case studies in this book. The first is the ways in which the dominant media has reported on what are popularly known as 'service delivery protests', mostly all involving poor communities. Largely, there is little to no interest in the actual grievances and/or demands that underlie the protests, and no attempt to talk to and engage the protestors. Rather, they are 'routinely covered only insofar as they present an inconvenience for the middle classes' (Wasserman 2017); and, one might add, to the extent they disrupt business and make those in/with political and economic power look bad.

It is no surprise that the core framing of such protests, as evidenced in Rebecca Pointer's 2013 survey study, consist of the 'war/spectacle frame and the failed democracy frame, followed by the law/crime frame, all of which serve to delegitimise service delivery protests' (Pointer 2015: 4). In

other words, what has been consciously constructed is a completely negative frame wherein the actions of the poor, in this case through protest
over the basics of life, are a priori something that is societally undesir-
able and disruptive of the 'normal' order of things. Within this frame, the
agency of the protestors is nullified as are the larger, systemic issues and
questions (for example, class inequality).

The second example is the Marikana massacre, which took place on
16 August 2012. As Jane Duncan (2013a: 65) has so cogently argued, the
dominant media's coverage, more especially in the immediate periods
leading up to and after the massacre, 'was heavily biased towards official
accounts … and … overwhelmingly favoured business sources … [who]
were the most likely to be primary definers of news stories' (see chapter 1).
This provided the platform for the dominant media 'to become a loudspeaker for powerful interests in the South African political and social-
economic nexus' wherein 'by and large, the journalistic principles of
fairness, balance, truth and ethics were neglected' (Rodny-Gumede 2015).

Very much like what has been shown to be the case in the three communities covered here, the privileging of elite voices (including those
voices that are not part of the elite but which have effectively been
captured by it), combined with the broader dissemination and reproduction of those voices through a range of other avenues, served to reinforce
a broader elitist narrative that the ideas and practices of those with political and economic power will always be the dominant ones. In the words
of Duncan (2013a: 80), the Marikana massacre 'provides a case study of
how reporting can become system-maintaining'.

This where the issue of elite dissemination and reproduction by those
who are in control of the state, the corporate sector, political parties and
even some civil society organisations (CSOs) comes into play – that
which is beyond the immediate reader or viewership of the dominant
print and audio-visual media. This can and does take place through
myriad ways, including advertisements, public statements, propaganda,
internal employee as well as sectoral communication and information,

public events (debates, discussions, speeches and marches), support for certain CSOs and, of course, regulations and policies.

In general terms, there is a coalescing of ideological views and narratives among elites precisely because they ultimately have common class interests. The most basic of those common interests is to make profit and accumulate capital (in different forms) and thus to defend and expand the capitalist market as the primary vehicle. Additionally, this works to ensure that the capitalist class, usually supported by the majority of the middle class, remains in political, administrative, social and economic charge of both the public and private sectors and key institutions within society. While the elites might not always agree with what the dominant media covers and produces (especially when it involves corruption, mismanagement, controversial racial, identity, sexual and other social issues, as well as the personal lives or problems of leaders and executives), when it comes to the big political and economic issues there is most often concrete or at least tacit agreement.

What elites fear the most is a loss of their class power and status. One of the most crucial means of defending and indeed strengthening that status and power has always been, and remains, winning the battle of ideas (George 1997) – how people see, understand and interpret the world around them and thus how they make their life choices and practically engage that world. In Julie Reid's (2016) accurate application of this to the media landscape, this 'ideological' terrain is hugely 'important, because it is here that media audience[s] not only acquire information about the world around them, but "decide" what to think (read, are encouraged how to think) about it'. This is why it is not just the dominant media itself that is central to such a battle but also the subsequent dissemination of the ideas that inform and frame the discourse and narrative of that dominant media.

It is not of ultimate importance to the elites, for example, whether some of the Glebelands hit men are eventually convicted and jailed; whether MRC's South African subsidiaries actually end up getting a licence to mine the Xolobeni sand dunes; or whether the majority of residents

of Thembelihle are finally evicted or not. What is of ultimate importance, though, is that each of these poor communities understands and
accepts that they do not have the power to call the shots, to decide their
overall developmental frame and path ahead, and to contest and defeat
the capitalists and their allies through whatever means. It is to that larger
political economy that we now turn our attention.

7

The Political Economy of Dominant Power and Storytelling

Dale T. McKinley

The ideas of the ruling class are in every epoch the ruling ideas, i.e. the class which is the ruling material force of society is at the same time its ruling intellectual force. The class which has the means of material production at its disposal has control at the same time over the means of mental production, so that thereby, generally speaking, the ideas of those who lack the means of mental production are subject to it.

— Marx and Engels, *The German Ideology*

SOCIETAL DOMINANCE: THEORY AND PRACTICE

To summarise the quote above from Marx and Engels for the purposes of the framing analysis here, the ideas of the ruling class (which consists of many different elements) are the dominant ideas in society. However, unlike an orthodox reading of Marx, such societal dominance is not always and everywhere maintained solely through the use of force but, as Antonio Gramsci (1971) posits, through the construction of a societal (or cultural) hegemony, in which consent of the masses is necessary.

Within what Gramsci broadly calls 'civil society', the ruling class is able to construct and maintain such hegemony (dominance), for example, through areas such as education and the media. Over time, the ideas about and practical ways (societal norms) in which the ruling class and the elites see and interpret the world become those of the masses themselves;[1] that is, they are inculcated, consented to and broadly legitimised. A dominant (ruling) class in society translates into dominant ideas, dominant institutions, dominant social forces, dominant sectors of the economy and dominant political parties.

To fully locate and understand this kind of multisided societal dominance in democratic South Africa, let's take a brief look at the practical frame within which it has developed. Almost coterminous with the African National Congress's (ANC's) rise to state power in 1994 was the adoption of a capitalist neo-liberal macroeconomic policy framework, which profoundly reshaped not only the political economy of South Africa but the more specific material realities and accompanying struggles of poor communities (Marais 1998).

For those communities, such as Glebelands and Thembelihle, the impacts were devastating. Massive job losses as well as widespread casualisation of labour were experienced by those fortunate enough to be employed; the 'experience' being accompanied by multifaceted social and economic damage to already vulnerable families and communities. In parallel, basic needs policies were implemented that turned many services, as well as much public/state land, into market commodities, facilitated by a drastic decrease in national government grants and subsidies to municipalities, as well as outsourced and privatised service delivery (McDonald 2002).

The combined results were a huge escalation in the costs of such services for the poor, as well as a consistent pattern of service cut-offs and evictions. This 'perfect storm' of neo-liberalism then laid the foundations for an enabling environment of patronage, corruption and factional politics, all overlaid with heavy doses of social and political conflict and violence. It was within this context that a range of new community organisations and social movements surfaced (Ballard, Habib and Valodia 2006; Naidoo and Veriava 2003). From the beginning, many of them (especially those emerging from poor communities) have been subject to a campaign by various elements of the ruling class of rhetorical vitriol, physical assaults and the general closing down of democratic voice and space (McKinley and Veriava 2010).

Over the last 20 years or so, this has produced a double 'movement' in respect of poor communities and their struggles. On the one hand, there is a hyper-commoditised daily existence where the vast majority of residents engage in a struggle for material survival as well as social inclusion, relevance and location. The result has been an intensification of division, stratification and dysfunction, now more than ever driven on by increasingly corrupt and conflict-ridden manoeuvring (involving both the public and private sectors) for limited social benefits, basic services and employment or productive opportunities.

On the other hand, there have been growing levels of tension and conflict that have manifested in various forms of local community protests and violence, most often involving the state's police forces, corporate actors (for example, mining companies), as well as local politicians and elites (Alexander 2010; Von Holdt 2013).

The kind of class warfare that such societal dominance has produced in post-apartheid South Africa has resulted in the broadening and deepening of structural inequality. Even though it is hard to imagine, South Africa is now more unequal than it was at the end of the apartheid era (Oxfam 2014). In 2013, aggregate wealth was estimated to be about R6.5 trillion, with 75 per cent being held by the top 10 per cent of South Africans (mostly in financial assets) and only 2.5 per cent being held by the bottom 50 per cent of the population (Simkins 2014).

A significant part of the reason why this extreme level of inequality has intensified is the continued ability of corporate capital to rely on cheap and productive black labour, more particularly that of black women. Even while the working conditions for many workers have improved since 1994, the overall share of wages in the South African economy as a percentage of gross domestic product declined from 57 per cent in 1994 to 50 per cent in 2011 (Simkins 2014).

When it comes to the more explicitly political/institutional side, what has transpired in democratic South Africa – through the ruling party – is part of a common thread that runs through all ex-national liberation movements that have come to political power across southern Africa after protracted struggles against various forms of colonialism. In myriad forms, the party (the ANC) has reproduced and then refashioned the elitist, narrowly nationalistic, parasitic and authoritarian colonial/apartheid lineage of power.

This has resulted in a gradual but systematic sidelining of a competing lineage of power emanating from the mass of people (the majority of whom are poor and black), which actually constituted the liberation movement. That lineage is one that is anti-colonial, independent, liberatory and democratic in both thought and practice and whose promise was, and remains, one of systemic political, social, economic and cultural change. The generalised 'triumph', at least up until the present, of the colonial lineage has thus produced a situation in which the ruling party has become the main vehicle for exercising a refashioned (if somewhat deracialised) societal dominance that reproduces the systemic economic and social power of the colonial/apartheid past (McKinley 2017).

It is within this overall frame that the presence, content and character, as well as practical role of a dominant media in South Africa – and here in specific reference to the coverage of poor communities in conflict – needs to be conceptualised and understood. Without it, the ability of the ruling class to sustain and strengthen its overall societal dominance would be severely compromised.

THE DIALECTICS OF DOMINANCE

There are many different understandings and definitions of what dialectics means (and how a dialectical method should be applied). Here, the most appropriate one is also one of the most simple: a 'medium that helps us comprehend a world that is racked by paradox … to arrive at the truth' (O'Connor 2003).

The paradox to which such application is required in respect of the societal dominance, of which the dominant media is an integral part, can be set out as follows: on the one hand, the ways in which it has rooted and shaped the developmental and indeed life possibilities and experiences of the communities, along with the consequent struggles and conflicts they have engaged, which frames how they/things are seen. On the other hand, the ways in which it has foundationally constructed a dominant thought frame and discourse (both in general terms and as applied to the relevant communities) that is largely defined by a complex but interrelated set of selective evidence, misrepresentations, lies and myths, which then serve self-interested/self-fulfilling motivations and assumptions.

The contemporary political, social and economic realities for the majority of people in South Africa provide more than enough evidence to confirm that the developmental path followed since 1994 has abjectly failed, in the words of the Freedom Charter, to 'meet the aspirations of exploited and oppressed people' (Congress of the People 1955). Like the global reality, the different components of the ruling class that drive the party-state-capital matrix of power and privilege in South Africa have been waging an unrelenting class war on the poor.

This has resulted in more and more people losing their jobs and homes and being forced into whatever precarious work they can find or create just to survive; the majority of an entire generation of youth cast aside as superfluous to the needs of the capitalist market; rural communities with few public services, some barely eking out a living on barren and poisoned land; poor inner-city residents crammed into hellhole tenements; and shack cities across the land where children play in open sewage, residents breathe in toxic air and people scavenge in rubbish dumps so they won't starve (McKinley 2017: 133).

In a world and country where dominance has become the living and experiential frame, the 'losers' are the poor. It is in communities like Glebelands, Xolobeni and Thembelihle that people are constantly told to be patient, while the elusive dream of a better life is held hostage to the whims and interests of the elites.

'As long as people play to this (dominance) script', there is nothing for the dominant media to report or comment on; indeed, there is 'nothing to see, precisely because there is no … recognition of anything that is "out of the ordinary"' (McKinley and Veriava 2007). It is when people do not accept the script that has been written for them, when they actively question and practically resist and disrupt, that the dominant media jumps into action. As confirmed in the resident/activist interviews, the resistance and disruption are one of the only ways in which poor communities can potentially 'draw the gaze' of the dominant societal forces (McKinley and Veriava 2007).

Whatever secondary criticisms there might be, the primary function and effect of subsequent coverage is to naturalise and normalise the dominant status quo, whether that be the constructed incompetence and indifference of government entities, the poor state of basic service and infrastructural delivery, the differential meting out of 'law and order' or the impunity with which private capital acts.

The developmental logic flowing from this is the reduction of poor communities to bare life, both materially and psychologically. In this frame, community development is usually deferred to the flow of market forces, outsourced to those who have no interest in anyone's welfare other than their own. In the process, the realities and truths of life and struggle are buried. If something is not seen then, for all intents and purposes, it becomes 'invisible', and that includes people themselves.

There are many pertinent examples to be taken from the interviews and media sampling in earlier chapters of this book. Here are three general examples taken from the three communities under discussion.

For the Glebelands community, the conflict has already developed to such extremes that the main focus for voice and struggle has become simply to be seen and heard. This is not merely applicable in relation to stopping the killings but has to do just as much with reclaiming self-esteem and equal citizenship. There is an acute awareness of the interconnectedness of the killings, the developmental state of Glebelands and the actions of those in/with power; and that the normalising of each – with the dominant media playing a central role – is what lies at the heart of their reality.

The community of Xolobeni/Amadiba is resolute in their applied rejection of 'modern' capitalist development, which follows a commodified, extractivist, competitive and individualistic path. Simultaneously, they are just as resolute in their advocacy of a historically grounded, organic, naturally connected and collective developmental path. It is this worldview and their concomitant actions that are directly coupled to how the forces of dominance, including most of the media, then see and deal with the community's rejection of their model, of their thinking and of their solutions. However, the community can see through the attempts to delegitimise and denigrate them as backward and as poor and to treat their resistance and struggles as a reactive aberration.

In Thembelihle, the negative perceptions of the community, in general, and of the actions of activists and protestors, in particular, matter a great deal. There is a clear understanding that these perceptions emanate principally from the coverage of the dominant media and have very practical consequences for how both the state authorities and the other classes respond to their voices and actions. As a result, there exists an enduring and gathering anger and frustration, which largely serves to widen the class divide, intensify conflict and fuel the desire for recognition and inclusion.

If there is one core point that materialises from all three cases, it is that the dominant media has for the most part played the role of, at best, one of the main facilitators of the dominance frame and, at worst, a key and proactive protagonist. The disconnect between this media and the poor communities is fundamentally to be found in a relationship that is defined by those who have and those who don't; those who are dominators and those who are the dominated.

When it comes to the construction and impact of a dominant thought frame and discourse in the more contemporary period in South Africa, it is necessary to reference the historical context within which it was born, nurtured and then 'naturalised' as part of a post-apartheid political economy. That context is the acceptance, legitimisation and pursuit of a societal dominance frame that was foundationally built on the systemic economic and social power of the colonial (apartheid) past.

By way of brief explanation: the democratic breakthrough in South Africa occurred in a national, continental and global context of highly unequal power relations that carried over the colonial dominance frame in very specific ways. While there was a political break from the past, the same did not happen on the economic, socio-psychological and cultural fronts. Borrowing from Indian political psychologist and sociologist Ashis Nandy's analysis of India's immediate post-independence period, this represents, 'a colonialism which survives the demise of empires' (1983: xi). More specifically, Nandy argues that 'the psychological and social hierarchies that enabled the West to harness its own productive capacities were re-imposed … this time entirely in the service of domination and denial' (in Wurgraft 1985: 435).

Applying this to South Africa, these hierarchies – of dominant socio-economic position and location, inclusive of and combining class, race, gender and sexuality, which were the pillars of the colonial dominance frame – were then superimposed onto the political 'rule' of the new South African state. Indeed, the very deal that facilitated the democratic transition was symbiotically tied to societal acceptance and inculcation of those hierarchies.

What has reinforced the durability of these hierarchies in post-1994 South Africa is that they fit neatly into the fundamentals of a capitalist neo-liberalism, which was and has remained the dominant global 'developmental' frame for the last 30-plus years and which was wholeheartedly embraced by South African capital and the new democratic state. The absolute societal dominance of the capitalist 'free market' that lies at the heart of neo-liberalism requires the political, social and ideological destruction of the possibilities of a different set of social relations and of alternative ideas for development.

Indeed, neo-liberalism carries with it tremendous 'pedagogical and ideological power' that seeks to control 'all of social life and not simply the market' (Giroux in Samalavicius 2016). As Pierre Bourdieu (1998) made so clear, the essence of neo-liberalism is about destroying the possibility of anything else; about destroying the aspirations, dreams and struggles of the vast majority of humanity; no more so than as applied to the poor.

The subsequent thought frame and discourse that has emerged from and been constructed around this neo-liberal frame has been and remains crucial to normalising the incredible inequalities that are now embedded into South Africa's contemporary political economy. For this normalisation to be sustained, there is the need to constantly reproduce and disseminate a storyline of inevitability; the inevitability of a structural inequality where there is always going to be a small minority of rich and a large majority of poor; the inevitability of economic and environmental exploitation; the inevitability of profit maximisation and corruption; the inevitability of racial, gender and sexual subjugation and discrimination; and the inevitability of a hyper-individualistic, consumerised and ultimately atomised way of living.

In turn, this inevitability storyline requires that the material realities and socio-psychological impacts (largely of/on the poor), which derive from its pursuit and implementation, are, in relative measure, obscured, manipulated, caricatured, patronised, mythologised, stereotyped and, when deemed necessary, ignored. This can be seen, for example, in constructing the lie that the majority of the people of Xolobeni/Amadiba area are in favour of the mining project, or casting the high levels of violence and death at Glebelands as primarily the result of personal and factional fights over room allocations.

But, beyond these very specific applications, the consequent storytelling is made much easier when applied to the residents of poor communities, such as those in Glebelands, Xolobeni/Amadiba and Thembelihle, precisely because they are, by and large, excluded from the dominant frame – that is, the 'mainstream' economy/capitalist market – as well as from parallel social relations. Put differently, they are effectively interlopers who are 'allowed' in when needed but for the most part are outsiders. They are a nuisance that needs to be dealt with when they get out of line (in different ways depending on the contextual realities and various political/social forces at play) and, if necessary, moved out of the main line of sight, whether symbolically or physically.

Those who live in these communities and the struggles that they wage are an unpredictable threat to the believability and thus continued effectiveness of the dominant storyline, as long as they are not under control and obedient. Since such control and obedience is highly unlikely in a situation of mass structural exclusion and inequality, the people and their communities have become (for the dominant societal forces, including the media as a whole) little more than useful tools to wage elitist political and social battles for power, position and financial gain, and objects of paternalistic pity and for the assuaging of (occasionally) damaged moral consciences.

At the foundational centre of the societal dominance frame sketched earlier is a media industry that has accepted and institutionalised a capitalist, neo-liberal-inspired and top-down political and ideological understanding of, and practical approach to, development and democracy. As a result, that (dominant) media is largely and consciously blind to seeing development and democracy as a metaphorical 'house' whose stability and habitability requires the laying of a foundation of basic socio-economic needs and services, participatory spaces, as well as spatial inclusivity and social dignity for the majority who live in it.

Because of that blindness, the enduringly unjust and unequal social and economic conditions of life for the poor (however much associated criticism is directed at the state for not doing a better job of ameliorating them), combined with the poor's response to those conditions, will forever be seen and treated as the main impediment to development and as the primary threat to democracy itself. In more representational terms, that blindness has completely skewed the real picture.

If subjected to full sightedness, that picture reveals that it is actually the other way around – that is, it is the very dominant frame of development and democracy that feeds and sustains those conditions and responses, and which thus poses the biggest threat to the stability and liveability of the entire edifice. In this sense, the dominant media plays an absolutely crucial role in propagating an elitist discourse and corresponding narrative that upholds and defends the very class privilege and resultant inequality, which gives rise to most of the societal problems and crises that provide the same media with the majority of their coverage material.

In the instructive words of Jane Duncan (2013a: 84):

> Two decades into democracy, the South African media still constitute an elite public sphere. This means that media discourses come to the South African public inherently unbalanced. Nothing short of a commitment to social justice, and to affirming society's most marginalised voices, will correct this imbalance. This … should mean going out of one's way to tell stories that those in positions of authority would prefer to remain buried. It also means recognising that those who are not in positions of authority are more likely to be bearers of these stories, and seeking them out.

PART 3

NEW TRAJECTORIES FOR JOURNALISM AND VOICE(S)

8

Media Diversity and Voice(s)

Julie Reid

Published in 1960, Harper Lee's novel *To Kill a Mockingbird* was immediately successful, and subsequently came to be considered one of the great classics of American literature. At the core of the book are themes of social justice and racial injustice. But it is the heart-wrenching unfairness when some people are both represented, as well as held to account, in ways that are blatantly inconsistent with other people, simply because of the power imbued in arbitrary descriptors such as race, class or social status that touches us. The mockingbird encompasses 17 different species of birds, which are known for the way in which their calls mimic other birds or insects.

In this section of this book, the mockingbird metaphor refers to dominant news media outlets that consistently mimic and reproduce content aligned to the same worldviews and ideological positioning, often at the expense of the ethical, moral and social justice implications of doing so.

While the task to transform the mainstream media into a sphere that is more willing and capable of operating as a platform for the wider inclusion of voice(s) is a moral, ethical and democratic project, it is also one that can positively impact on the financial bottom line of media outlets. All over the world, and in South Africa, the news media currently faces a double-edged crisis: a crisis of credibility and a crisis of financial sustainability (the latter is particularly hard felt by the print media sector). We will address the financial sustainability aspect a little later, but first the matter of credibility, which for any legitimate news media outlet is and ought to be its most prized possession.

Political and social discourse surrounding what is now called fake news is partly fed by genuine concern for the factual accuracy of the news, but also partly by moral panic, part hysteria, a large part by political actors as a means of directing attention away from their own failings and scapegoating the media, and partly because fake news in the post-digital age becomes increasingly easier to produce, replicate and disseminate. Importantly, misinformation, in one form or another, has been with us for as long as the mass communications media has formed part of our daily lives. We used to call it things like propaganda, unethical journalism, plagiarism, brown-envelope journalism or spin doctoring.

Traditionally, democratic societies have established regulatory bodies, such as press councils or complaints commissions, to monitor errant journalism and offer a means of media accountability by sanctioning media outlets when these are found to have breached a predetermined code of ethics. The regulatory difficulties associated with the phenomenon of fake news, however, are not as easy to handle. Firstly, fake news is not simply false news, inaccurate reporting or lazy journalism, which would fall into the usual jurisdiction of ethics bodies such as press councils. Instead, it is purposefully manufactured according to a particular political imperative, often as part of a consciously constructed campaign that aims to reach a predetermined political result. The proliferation of fake news can also be overwhelming in scale when a deliberate lie is picked up by numerous blogs, or reiterated by hundreds of websites, shared and cross-posted across multiple social media platforms and consumed by thousands of media users (UNESCO 2018). It is a media regulator's nightmare.

Problematically, the knock-on effect of this is that the mainstream media inadvertently suffers a significant dent in credibility. This is not entirely fair. While some media outlets have fallen foul, and – possibly as a result of inadequate fact-checking – have reproduced fake news content, we already know that a significantly large quantity of fake news in circulation is initiated by governments or political actors, motivated by political imperatives, such as swinging elections or damaging the reputation of opponents (Posetti 2018a). This is coupled with an increasing and substantial trend of conscious delegitimisation of the news media, largely caused by sustained and systematic attacks on the media by government actors.

Today, government representatives and spokespeople regularly trivialise and insult the media, sometimes characterising it as the 'enemy', in ways that would have been unthinkable just a few years ago in democratic societies, and which would have undoubtedly drawn vehement criticism with regard to the implications on the freedom of the press and media independence. But political leaders now swat critical news stories aside with relative ease, simply by referring to them as fake news (UNESCO 2018). Not only does this kind of delegitimisation reinforce attacks on the media by other sections of society, but the often misguided messaging of these campaigns is heard by thousands of people, and no doubt believed by some.

As a result, the news media's credibility suffers, which is only compounded when combined with the already legitimate grievances of large swathes of society that the media routinely offers these people no 'voice', no representivity and habitually ignores stories from the ground. Where a majority of people already harbour a bitterness towards the dominant news media for its treatment of their stories and communities, it is unlikely that such audiences would be persuaded to nonetheless retain faith in the news in the era of the fake news phenomenon. This then becomes an inconvenient toxic mix for the dominant press:

audiences who did not trust the media to begin with (for reasons that can be laid squarely at the door of the mainstream media) are unlikely to treat the fake news conundrum faced by the media today with much compassion, regardless of whether the fake news phenomenon is of the mainstream news media's making or not.

But it is also a toxic mix for participatory democracy, the effectiveness of which relies on an informed citizenry. In simple terms, it is important that people do indeed believe what they see in the news, reliant, of course, on the prerequisite that news content is fair, accurate, balanced and, well, not fake. The academic field of media diversity studies, as well as media lawmakers and regulators (in democratic countries and institutions at least), have long reached consensus that media diversity is a crucial aspect of the information landscape and vital to the health of a robust democracy. The precise nature of the notion of media diversity is widely theoretically contested (Duncan and Reid 2013; Karppinen 2007).

But leaving aside the highly complex nuts and bolts of media diversity theory, one basic normative premise prevails almost universally among researchers, media rights activists and, importantly, multilateral, inter-national and (democratic) governmental media-orientated groupings and law-making initiatives. This means that the diversity of content in the media is important to society and democracy, and should reflect the widest possible range of cultural and political ideas, because the media is integral to each individual's formulation of personal opinions, ideas and worldview (Duncan and Reid 2013). A diverse media landscape is one that provides each media user with access to a broad spectrum of information, political orientations and cultural practices, so that the indi-vidual is able to freely determine their own position within the political world and decide how and when to participate in that world.

The idea is simple enough: access to a variety of ideas and informa-tion is a good thing. It is also why when authoritarian regimes inhibit the spectrum of content available in a country's media it is considered a violation of the freedoms and information rights of its citizens, as is the case in countries such as North Korea, for example, and, to some extent,

China. But even in mature or developing democracies, acceptable and sustainable levels of media diversity are not always easily achieved.

The most prominent inhibitor of media diversity in democratic societies is the over-concentration and monopolisation of media markets. Thinking in business terms, as cultural artefacts, media products bear a high risk of failure. Larger media conglomerates are able to mitigate these risks: if one media product proves unpopular, such failure can be covered and financed off the profitability of more successful products. Smaller media companies and new entrants are less able to afford or withstand product failure, and face a much higher degree of risk. Resultantly, media systems are often dominated by large monopolies and an unpluralistic ownership pattern, where a small collection of media owners produce, disseminate and control the majority of media content (Duncan and Reid 2013; Van Cuilenburg 2007).

What this means for the ordinary audience member is that although one might have access to a reasonable variety of programmes, channels and/or newspapers, these are all produced by the same company and therefore potentially all bear a similar ideological orientation. This is far from ideal with respect to gaining the widest possible access to a broad range of opinions and ideas. Here, the media diversity principle fails in practice.

In various countries, this has prompted lawmakers to discuss or attempt market intervention, and South Africa is not an exception. Between September 2011 and March 2012, the South African Parliamentary Portfolio Committee on Communications hosted a series of discussions on transformation and diversity within the print media sector (Duncan and Reid 2013). African National Congress (ANC) Portfolio Committee members argued in favour of the development of a print media transformation charter, which was reiterated in the party's 53rd national conference resolutions in December 2012, then framing the notion as an 'economic empowerment charter to promote Broad Based Black Economic Empowerment in the sector' (ANC 2012: 63). These sentiments were again echoed by the then minister of communications,

Faith Muthambi, and the Universal Service and Access Agency of South Africa CEO, Lumko Mtimde (formerly the head of the Media Development and Diversity Agency), at the Print Media Transformation Colloquium in August 2016, which was organised by the Department of Communications (Reid 2016).

Unfortunately, the answer to this media diversity conundrum is not as simple as ensuring a plurality of media ownership. The support of new entrants and/or the breaking up of media monopolies can have a ruinous effect on the media system in its entirety. When the number of media outlets within a particular media market increases, each separate outlet then naturally captures a smaller portion of the audience. As the audience fragments across different outlets, the profitability of each outlet diminishes, meaning that less expensive and lower quality content is then offered by the outlet, which in turn reduces the outlet's audience and income (Van Cuilenburg 2007). Large parts of the media system in this scenario are then caught in a downward spiral.

The situation can be somewhat rescued by something called Hotelling's law of excessive sameness. A greater number of media outlets within a media system results in a highly competitive market and homogeneity of content often results, where competing media outlets try to imitate the content offered by their competitors. Under conditions of such fierce competition, the social and democratic importance of providing a broad spectrum of diverse content is superseded by each media outlet's battle to remain financially sustainable in a highly competitive environment. This situation is also detrimental to experimentation, since, again, media outlets are less able to financially withstand the risk associated with more innovative products, and rely more heavily on the tried and tested and already proven to be popular products (Duncan and Reid 2013; Van Cuilenburg 2007). In other words, audiences are fed more of the same by a wider number of media outlets.

While all of this goes some way to preventing the complete ruin of the media market, and superficially preserves the financial sustainability of media outlets, it does not offer much help in providing the population of media users with access to a broad spectrum of diverse ideas, opinions and worldviews. Combating the over-concentration of a media market by encouraging the start-up of new entrants and the breaking up of monopolies can potentially result in degrees of excessive sameness that actually see audiences worse off than they were before, with regard to their mediated levels of exposure to varying opinions, ideas and views. In light of the above, and although the South African media market is somewhat concentrated in ownership structure, with the state-owned South African Broadcasting Corporation (SABC) operating as the biggest monopoly in terms of audience figures, it has to be borne in mind that an already financially strained media market as small as South Africa's would likely struggle to withstand interventions in the market by government, however well-intentioned these may be.

FREE THE MOCKINGBIRD: INCLUSIVE MEDIA DIVERSITY

But a middle way remains to alleviate the media diversity problem, and one that is given scant attention by media policymakers, media researchers and the media sector itself. What if, for example, existing media outlets could in fact provide satisfactory levels of media content diversity regardless of the ownership structure of the market (whether monopolistic in nature or diversified)? The adage often reiterated within South African media political discourse, most often spoken by government officials or representatives of the ANC party as a justification for the 'transformation of the South African print sector' is 'he who pays the piper, calls the tune'. This is meant to connote that media owners too often determine the ideological and political trajectory of the news media outlets falling within their stable. While it is difficult to empirically prove a direct correlation between the owners of a media outlet and the nature of that outlet's content, the South African news media has long been observed and critiqued for presenting little but a middle-class bias and the narrow interests of the societal elite (Friedman 2011). These same criticisms are echoed and demonstrated in chapters 3–6 of this book.

However, it is short-sighted to believe that the only way in which to combat the lack of diversity within the media sphere is an overhaul in ownership structures. Of course, monopolies operating in environments of weak regulation are not a good thing, and can have adverse effects on the media sphere that stretch beyond media diversity concerns. The average cost to the media user of gaining access to media products is an example: many South Africans are denied access because the under-regulated, exorbitantly high costs and the profiteering practices of media and telecommunications companies mean that meaningful access to the media sphere costs more than what the majority of users can afford (Abrahams and Pillay 2014; Duncan and Reid 2013; Reid 2017a).

Nonetheless, a fine balance needs to be struck between preventing the over-concentration of the media market, the support and sustain-ability of new media entrants without initiating the spiralling effect or the law of sameness, and the promotion of media diversity within already existing, well-financed and economically sustainable media outlets. Regarding the latter, 'he or she who pays the media piper, does not necessarily have to call the tune'. This may at first sound unrea-sonable, but it is certainly not impossible. For instance, research from the Netherlands indicates that while the Dutch newspaper market is highly concentrated in terms of ownership, the very small number of publishers nonetheless caters for a significant degree of content diversity (Van Cuilenburg 2007). In democratic societies we should consider it entirely unacceptable that an investigative newspaper, for example, ought to mimic the ideological, political, economic class bias or orientations of its owners. News media outlets should not be mockingbirds and, where they are, they ought to be freed, at the very least with regard to the tune they wish to sing.

If we are able, in both theory and practice, to detach the influence of media ownership from the ideological orientation of news media con-tent, and accept that the former should not (and assure that in practice it does not) determine the latter, then we are free to open up a realm of new possibilities regarding the promotion of media diversity.

The influence that media owners exert on news media content has been discussed here because it forms the founding principle in the arguments of many media policy-and lawmakers, both abroad and within South Africa, who treat it as an infallible truth of fact and as justification enough to interfere in the ownership structure of the media market. Of course, many working within the media sector regularly reject the suggestion that they are somehow puppeteered by the owners of the outlet that employs them. That may be fair, but as various research efforts have shown, including the work conducted for this book, media workers, journalists and editors are certainly puppeteered by *something*.

If they were not, then the consistent characteristics of exclusion and sameness prevalent in the South African media landscape would not be so regularly confirmed by research studies that are conducted independently of one another (see, for example, Berger 2003; Duncan 2012; Friedman 2011; Garman and Malila 2017; Malila 2013, 2014; Malila and Garman 2016; Reid 2012; Wasserman 2013, 2017; Wasserman, Chuma and Bosch 2016). If South African journalists and editors did not mimic, and sing the tune of, to and for a singular segment of society so faithfully, then the voices of the various other peoples who live in the country could be more regularly heard.

We propose here a three-step formula for the promotion of media content diversity that dominant media outlets can adopt. It involves increasing levels of media content diversity by doing one simple thing: including the perspectives, views, ideas, opinions, stories and voice(s) of the people who are most unheard within the mediated sphere. The first step is to identify the voices and perspectives that are already heard, already covered and represented well by any particular outlet. The second step is to look for, listen out for and actively listen to the voice of the unheard. The third step involves the sensitive representation and inclusion of these voices in a participatory process of listening. We call this inclusive media diversity.

The concept of inclusive media diversity offers a new take on more traditional understandings of media diversity, where the latter routinely measure media diversity only with respect to the plurality of ownership within media markets, the availability of the number of media outlets and, in terms of content, limits assessments to superficial content diversity involving the adequate representations of race, ethnicity, gender, language and so on. While these factors are important, the above-mentioned aspects of representation can be thought of as a type of first-level content diversity. Inclusive media diversity considers also the second level of representation, which is not limited to the equal representation of languages, genders and ethnicities, but also concerns the diversity of voice(s). We use the term 'voice(s)' here to refer to the different cultural, socio-economic and political views and perspectives of the many predominantly under-represented segments of society. This second-level diversity is ideological in nature, but at its core is the concern for the availability and representation of a wide spectrum of voice(s) within a highly fragmented society.

This is where things can become complex. It is precisely because this second-level diversity is ideological in nature that implementing such media diversity can run up against the ideological slant of not only those who own the dominant media but also of a large number of those who work and write for that same media. An enabling environment for the germination and growth of inclusive media diversity is required, which can in part be assisted by the adoption of listening journalism. Notably though, the benefits of promoting inclusive diversity in dominant media practice are immense, both for the media sector itself, as well as the broader democratic environment. Giving more space, attention and voice to segments of society who have until now been habitually ignored by the dominant media contributes to alleviating the diversity problem. The inclusion of such voice(s) will naturally increase the degree of media content diversity offered by the dominant media sphere, giving more people more access to a much broader spectrum of ideas, opinions and worldviews, which is at the heart of the democratic media diversity ideal.

But there is more. People who see themselves in the media naturally take an interest in the media. Here, two things unfold. The first is that when more people have more interest in the media as an information source, a more informed citizenry results. Access to reliable information is not only key to overall development, education, economic growth and the practising of citizens' rights, but it also fosters an environment where people are able to respond to the political (social and economic) scenarios of the day in an informed way. So, it is good for democratic participation. Secondly, when people see themselves in the media, when they resultantly take an interest in the media, and when the media thereafter becomes an integral part of their lives and a key informant for how they move through the political world, the media becomes precious to them. This is the kind of media that people are willing to believe and, if needs be, protect. Making such connections to the ordinary citizen is key to alleviating the crisis of credibility suffered by the news media at present.

When people begin to see their own stories and hear about their own concerns and interests in the media, they become far more likely to participate as regular media users. The equation is so simple that it seems unnecessary to spell it out: the audience base of the media sector broadens and grows, making media products more profitable and media outlets more financially successful (especially with regard to privately owned and corporate media). A prerequisite of addressing the crisis of financial sustainability currently experienced by much of the media sector is the growth of the audience. It is therefore in the dominant media's own economic self-interest to broaden its representation of voice(s).

Actors within the dominant media will undoubtedly consider such an avenue unprofitable and therefore not worth the trouble. As we have seen repeatedly, the media is unlikely to uphold its (often self-proclaimed) social responsibility of representing the diversity of all communities that they serve if it is more lucrative to produce content that aligns to the interests of certain isolated segments of the audience (Plaisance 2009). This is a small-minded tactic and short-sighted when considering the benefits of growing the media audience, but also reveals a lack of engagement on the part of the dominant media with working-class and grassroots peoples on how they feel about the media sector. When we were conducting the series of interviews for this book, it became clear to us that people from poor and grassroots communities felt that they had legitimate grievances with the dominant press. These grievances were confirmed by our subsequent media content analysis. However, those same community residents also expressed an explicit understanding of the value of the media and its centrality as a means of communicating their struggles to the world.

For example, Sibusiso Mqadi has lived in the Amadiba region for most of his life. He has spent some time in the urban metropole of Durban and travelled throughout the country. However, he expressly prefers the community-orientated living in the rural setting of his picturesque home, which has long been under threat of being indelibly changed by a prospecting mining company. During our engagement with him, he related some examples of when he had been interviewed by journalists from the mainstream press on the struggles affecting his community. To his dismay, when he read the resultant reporting, he was disappointed at the inaccuracies and misrepresentations that the news articles contained. In his view, the journalists got it wrong. He also felt that although he had been interviewed, he had not been *heard*. In one of the last questions we asked, we requested that he relate to us what he would wish for his home region, what his dreams were for Xolobeni. He said, 'My first dream … is to win this mine thing, that is my first dream, is to win … which means maybe I can sleep well at night. And also, yes, as I said, to upgrade the tourism. And also a signal, to have a signal pole here' (X9 interview).

I was struck by his answer. In order to understand why, you need to be cognisant of the context. Xolobeni is located so deep within the Amadiba region that it is particularly isolated geographically from the closest town and the comforts that urban or town living offers. The dirt roads are badly maintained, pitted and potholed, making travel even in a 4×4 vehicle extremely difficult and in a standard car virtually impossible. The homes are humble, built by the hands of the families that reside in them. Very few structures in the area enjoy things like electricity or tapped running water. According to Western normative thinking, the area and its people would be considered the poorest of the poor. But residents, who for centuries have lived off their rugged land and for whom the understanding of wealth is conceptualised differently, do not think of themselves as poor. I was nonetheless amazed at Sibusiso's simple dream.

The 'signal pole' Sibusiso refers to is a terrestrial cellular transmission tower to capacitate better cellphone and data services in the area. It is not that Xolobeni does not receive cellular signals at all, just that these are very bad. The area does not have a cellular transmission tower of its own. In the time that we spent there, whenever Dale and I wanted to call home or check our email on our cellphones, we had to hike up to the summit of a nearby mountain to try to catch whatever meagre signal we could pick up from transmission towers many kilometres away.

Sibusiso could have wished for anything: tarred roads, electricity to his home, or any range of better municipal services, like water or health care. But he chose instead a cellphone tower. This speaks volumes to the value he places in accessing information, news and communication, and the desire he has to communicate himself. Sibusiso clearly understands the value of being connected, so much so that he expressed it as part of his precious dream. This is the spirit of the aspirant media user.

Where the dominant news media has represented the communities of the poor, marginalised, isolated and oppressed, it has, the world over, stereotyped, framed and mythologised them as criminals, uneducated, and with a barbaric propensity for violence (see, for example, Bullock, Fraser Wyche and Williams 2001). Nothing could be further from the truth, both in more general terms and in our experience of the communities we worked with for this study: in all three contexts we were welcomed with kindness by people who clearly had a rational and highly informed view of the troubles besetting their home region. And all of them had important stories to tell.

All three of the communities have been the sites of events and struggles that are undeniably newsworthy. Crucial events and developments have been under-reported or ignored entirely by the dominant media. In all three contexts, where the dominant media has reported stories relating to these communities, these reports have characteristically stereotyped community dwellers and rarely included space for voice(s) other than the dominant voice of officialdom.

These communities have justifiable grievances with the media. The interviewees related examples to us of their frustrations when they read news reports, which had, in their view, simply got the story wrong (in some cases by the omission of facts that community members had alerted journalists to). This does not mean that they do not want to be participants in the media sphere, only that they want the dominant media to work better for them. Over and above the motivations of fostering greater degrees of media content diversity, and of combating the media's crisis of both credibility and financial sustainability, the importance of enacting inclusive diversity of voice(s) is at its core a moral and an ethical necessity.

As described in chapter 7, in the dialectics of dominance, arbitrary descriptors such as race, class or economic status inevitably place some in positions of undue power as opposed to the majority who possess little power at all. When the dominant mockingbird media gives voice to the former while ignoring the latter, it simply parallels the societal structure of the world. But according to its societal responsibility and ethical mandate, it ought to do more than that. The question now is twofold: how to break the cage and free the mockingbird, and how do we ensure that it remains uncaged. The second question will be dealt with in the following chapter on media ethics and voice; the first question in the last chapter on planting the seeds of change.

Rethinking Media Freedom, Revamping Media Ethics

Julie Reid

> If journalism is a force of immense influence –
> and I think it is, and should be – then it surely deserves scrutiny.
> — Alan Rusbridger, former editor-in-chief of *The Guardian*

CRITIQUE IS NOT A CRIME

In a manner that resembles an almost automatic knee-jerk reaction, news media sector representatives, journalists and editors often respond to criticism of the press with assertions that the freedom and independence of the news media must be protected at all costs. For many, the freedom of the press is an infallible sacred cow. This line of argument is sometimes well placed, but at other times it is decidedly manipulative and unhelpful.

There is no question that the world's investigative news media suffers significant strain, resulting in part from the difficulties of financial sustainability and the crisis of credibility associated with delegitimisation campaigns and fake news. But it is also becoming increasingly more dangerous to be a journalist, especially for women. Direct threats to journalists, such as assassinations, death threats and intimidation, arrests and detention, or online trolling, are on the increase across the world. Political and governmental interference in the editorial independence of news outlets, politically connected media ownership and regulatory or legislative restrictions on freedom of expression and access to information are still prevalent in many countries, even in the second decade of the twenty-first century. The killing of journalists for reasons related to their investigative work is on the rise globally, and these cases are rarely investigated properly by the authorities. The resultant impunity means that the killers literally get away with murder (Posetti 2018b; UNESCO 2018).

Within this global context, it is easy to understand why journalists and media professionals automatically take up defensive positions when confronted with critiques of the profession. Journalists feel as though they are under attack, and they are. However, too often genuine critique and/ or evidence-based scrutiny of the news media's performance by media analysts is unreasonably equated with the tack of the sinister forces who intend to do media workers serious harm. But the two cannot simply be equated, and to tar them with the same brush, so to speak, is unfair. The rantings of a crooked politician who dismisses the news media's reportage as fake news, and calls for draconian media regulations in order to conceal his own corruption is one thing. The critique and criticisms of media analysts, but more especially of ordinary citizens, whose only request is that the news media works better for them, is an entirely different matter and ought to be respected. Threats against the freedom of the press may be serious, but they are not the same thing as genuine and constructive criticism that aims to contribute to a more democratised media sphere, and one that operates to serve its audience better. While these two factors ought to be considered separately, they are often argumentatively lumped into the same category, effectively nullifying any meaningful consideration of the latter.

The cherished ideal of journalistic independence and the often misdirected defence of this ideal denies the possibility of crucial interactions regarding the concept of accountability. Thus, the loud defence of the journalistic ideal prompts the question: independent from what and from whom? Surely not from the equally important journalistic ideals of fairness, balance and impartiality (Plaisance 2009)? And further, surely not from those whom the mainstream press professes to 'serve': the mediated public, the media audience and ordinary citizens?

The line of argument adopted by news practitioners within media-related discourse the world over, infused with connotations that the press ought to remain beyond reproach and untouchable in order to protect media freedom, has often proven unhelpful. This cop-out discoursal manoeuvre is not only irrational and unjustifiable, but is also an injustice to the billions of people who are media users, many of whom have legitimate grievances with the press. The freedom of the press is important, and of course it must be protected. But the freedom of everybody else and of ordinary citizens is also important, and it too should be taken into consideration.

Freedom of expression debates that focus solely on the freedom of expression rights of media workers can be a hindrance when they effectively block conversations about the freedom of expression and representation rights of media users and citizens. The right of freedom of expression of the press is traditionally regarded as universally so precious that any 'meddling' in content, despite the inherently problematic nature of that content, is widely regarded as patently wrong. This simplistic and naive view relegates the notion of media freedom to the role of a beating stick to dissuade anyone from suggesting that news media content needs to improve or change. It immediately disenables legitimate debate and introspection on the part of the media sector, thereby dismissing opportunities to explore new ways of creating media content that speaks to, for and about ordinary media users. But contrary to the way in which it has been mythologised, the freedom of the press is not a magic wand that imbues the news media with the status of an untouchable golden calf. The press can be critiqued without its rights being infringed upon, just like anything else.

For these reasons, among others, I have argued elsewhere for a substantial revision of the popular way in which we collectively think of the notion of media freedom (Reid 2017a). In summary, our definition of media and press freedom needs to change because of the current exclusionary nature of the popular understandings of these terms. Much of the debate on media accountability has centred on the tension that this causes between journalistic autonomy and the public's need for a responsible press (Plaisance 2009). However, if we were to understand media freedom differently, then this relationship may involve less tension and more balance.

MEDIA FREEDOM FOR A FEW

The now naturalised and traditional understanding of media and press freedom, at the simplest semiotic level, connotes only a concern for the impediments on media workers to perform their journalistic work with a satisfactory degree of independence and without unreasonable interference. Simply put.

In media policy and political discourse, the terms media and press freedom can be collectively and very generally summarised as pointing to rights of media workers and producers, editors and journalists to produce and disseminate media content freely, and without interference or fear of interference from the centres of power, whether that be: 1) the government, political actors, organs of the state; 2) corporates, big business, including but not exclusively media owners; or 3) in some countries, criminal elements, warlords, terrorist organisations or drug cartels (Reid 2017a: 78).

It is not that this definition of media freedom is necessarily wrong, but rather that it is not enough. Problematically, this definition only concerns itself with the rights and freedoms of media producers, and in a decidedly top-down fashion. But there are others who are entitled to enjoy media and communications rights and freedoms too: they may not be media producers or journalists themselves, but that does not mean that they do not aspire to the fulfilment of their media rights. The traditional application of media freedom as relevant to the rights of media producers only is also entirely out of symmetry with the multidimensional architecture of the media sphere. The most basic of communications models taught to undergraduate university students lays out the messaging chain as one that involves the 1) sender (journalists/media workers); 2) the disseminated content; and then 3) the receiver (the news media audience). While this pattern is overly simplistic and now outdated, the traditional definition of the term 'media freedom' does not align properly with even this simple model.

This is because the traditional definition of media freedom concentrates primarily on the rights and freedoms of the producers of media content only, and thus gives attention only to the first part of the model while ignoring the rest. This only covers one singular part of what is essentially a multilayered phenomenon. The communicative chain of media messaging does not end with the journalist. Once content is produced, it is disseminated, it arrives, it is consumed by media users, and in a post-digital age it is shared, reposted and often responded to, sometimes by citizen journalists and bloggers who then in turn begin a new cycle of related content production and dissemination (Reid 2017a). Accordingly,

> [i]f the idea of media freedom is applied to media producers only, with no regard to the audience, then only a small part of the mass communications chain is being considered, while what is, in a digital world, arguably the more crucial part, is being ignored. The entirety of the media chain does not only involve media producers, but includes the audience, so the notion of media freedom needs to be applied to the whole chain, not only part of it (Reid 2017a: 79).

Recognising that media freedom involves the rights of those beyond media producers only results in the necessary acknowledgement of those rights. Firstly, and also traditionally, media freedom, of course, involves the rights of media workers and journalists to 'speak' independently and without undue interference, also popularly called freedom of expression. But further to this are the rights of the other key nodal participants who are also involved in the mass communications chain, and, indeed, without whom the chain would collapse. The rights of media users and the audience involve the freedom of access to the media, without facing undue barriers to access.

Open access to information rights are often impeded, for example, due to the high costs involved in accessing media content, among various other factors. Joining the dots here naturally results in the inclusion of the right to a varied range of media content according to the democratic ideal of media diversity. Further, media audience rights include the right to respond to media content, whether via social media platforms or otherwise, which forms a different though equally crucial site for freedom of expression. The rights of the media audience and the public also includes a right of representivity, of voice, or the right to have one's story told in a dignified, accurate and respectful manner, including what Charles Husband (1996, 2008) calls the right to be understood. Media freedom, then, is not as simple as it seems.

Redefining a term like 'media freedom', which is now so acutely entrenched in media related discourse, is one thing. Popularising this redefinition, and, moreover, operationalising it in some more practical way, is another. But 'a semiotic project of consciously counter-mythologising the popularised yet over-simplified definition of "media freedom", which currently displays a fundamental poverty of complexity … is both a moral and an ethical one', most especially because of the pursuit of audience-centredness and the consideration of a broader spectrum of rights (Reid 2017a: 90–91). Naturally then, we turn to the realm of media ethics.

MEDIA ETHICS AND MEDIA ACCOUNTABILITY REFORM

The 'right to be understood', as a loosely formulated listening-related concept, emerged only a few years ago as a part of discussions aimed at destabilising conventional Western-orientated communicative power, and as an affront to the Western media's obstinacy in the face of demands for reform from the global South. Today, we would view this as part of the efforts of the broader movement of decolonisation. Stemming from his prior experience of the 1980s struggle for a new world information and communication order, Husband argued for the recognition of a collective right to be understood and heard. This right was envisaged as a much more meaningful reform than those related to individualistic rights, such as those 'to utter, to publish, to broadcast, [and] to consume' that were common then, and still are (Husband 2008). Husband maintained that a key determinant of democratic, dialogic communication was the precondition of acknowledgement from those with media access and production power that they had an obligation to listen in equal measure to the right of the world's poor to speak and be heard (Husband 2008; O'Donnell, Lloyd and Dreher 2009).

This obligation to listen, and the right to speak and be heard, is considered more contextually by Herman Wasserman (2013), who argues for an 'ethics of listening'. Here it is important that journalists do not remain immune to the contextual socio-political realities and the everyday lived conditions of citizens, but instead consciously acknowledge these as a means to break the mould, which determines that particular segments of society hold unequitable means and power to make themselves heard in the public sphere (Wasserman 2013: 77).

While South Africa, as a new democracy, remains a highly fragmented and unequal society, the concept of 'listening' provides an ethical basis that is an alternative to dominant normative frameworks of both accountability and storytelling (Wasserman 2013). Wasserman (2013: 77) contends 'that "listening" as an ethical value is appropriate for a new democracy where social polarisations continue to impact media narratives and agendas, and in a society where continued economic inequalities provide certain parts of the citizenry with disproportionate power to make themselves heard in the public sphere. To treat people with dignity primarily means taking their stories seriously.'

Listening, as an ethical value in journalistic practice, is then additionally connected to the right of human dignity, and the equitable distribution of this right. For the mainstream press to cater to more than the interests and motivations of an elite, journalists need to learn the skill of listening, more broadly, more sensitively and with more respect. It would involve active and purposeful listening to those who most often find themselves on the periphery of the public sphere, rather than at its centre. By listening to the stories of the marginalised, by respecting their authority over their own stories and how they narrate their own lives, the ethics of listening becomes key to material dignity (Wasserman 2013).

On an even more practical level, the ethics of listening is not just about dignity, but also about some of the more time-honoured ideals of professional journalism, such as accuracy, fairness, truthfulness and balance. For a profession that places extremely high value on credibility, no reliable journalist would argue against the importance of getting the facts right (as far as is reasonably possible), of offering a fair and true depiction of events, and presenting the narration of a story in a balanced way. But without a consideration of voice, without actively seeking out the voice(s) indelibly connected to a story, and without the practice of the ethics of listening, are fairness, balance and/or accuracy even possible?

In many democratic countries, including South Africa, the media sector has accepted, albeit sometimes begrudgingly, the establishment of voluntary media accountability systems, such as press councils or complaints commissions. These institutions are primarily responsible for formulating predetermined codes of ethics or conduct, to which media outlets may voluntarily subscribe, and which offer somewhat rigid sets of guidelines for good journalistic practice. The assumption here is that the media should do no unnecessary harm, and codes of ethics can cover a wide range of aspects of reporting, including the prohibition of misleading headlines, the responsibility of media outlets to allow for a right of reply, care to be taken when reporting on vulnerable people, such as children or victims of sexual violence, and so on.

Almost universally, codes of media ethics contain a set of what I call the 'first principles', from whence all other provisions in the code take their lead. The first principles generally dictate that news reporting ought to be a fair representation of events, only report that which can be considered reasonably true, do not involve a departure from the facts, and contain balance in order to represent the varying perspectives on any particular story. The first principles are the foundational concepts of the field of news media ethics, and guide the practical implementation of regulatory accountability carried out by media complaints bodies. We will return to these first principles later.

The institution of the Press Council of South Africa (PCSA) has undergone a nearly continuous process of review and restructuring for the past decade, and on each occasion this has been accompanied by a revision of the code of ethics for South African print and digital news media journalists. Indeed, as this is being written, another newly revised code of ethics was introduced by the PCSA in January 2019. This media accountability mechanism has been subjected to regular public scrutiny, often and admirably of its own volition when the PCSA has invited public commentary on its procedures, and also once at the hands of an independent enquiry, the Press Freedom Commission (Reid 2014). For the most part, each of these various processes of review have resulted in positive changes to the press code, and structural improvements to the PCSA as an accountability mechanism, which have made this institution more accessible to the reading public, as well as improved the overall effectiveness and functioning of the press ombudsman's office (Reid and Isaacs 2015).

The organic flexibility of the PCSA, largely owing to the fact that it is not a statutory institution, makes possible this continuous cycle of improvement and allows the body to respond quickly to new regulatory challenges as they arise, which they often do, most especially within the realm of digital news publishing. Marc Caldwell (2011), however, mentions that many of the reflections and debates on current codes of ethics tend to emphasise rational procedures or the nuts and bolts of how to hold errant journalism to account in a logical way that corresponds to a predetermined set of rules. But the practical enactment of ethics from this view, and its accompanying accountability systems, focus so much on the rules that these measures become overly concerned with ensuring that journalism does no harm, rather than imagining how it could actually do some good (Caldwell 2011). This is a fair comment. How then could media accountability mechanisms be revised in a practical way to encourage a journalism that does some good? Let us return to the first principles.

As an example, the first principles in the PCSA's (2016) 'Press Code of Ethics and Conduct for South African Print and Online Media' read as follows:

1 Gathering and reporting of news

1.1 The media shall take care to report news truthfully, accurately and fairly.

1.2 News shall be presented in context and in a balanced manner, without any intentional or negligent departure from the facts whether by distortion, exaggeration or misrepresentation, material omissions, or summarisation.

1.3 Only what may reasonably be true, having regard to the sources of the news, may be presented as fact, and such facts shall be published fairly with reasonable regard to context and importance. Where a report is not based on facts or is founded on opinion, allegation, rumour or supposition, it shall be presented in such manner as to indicate this clearly.

A similar example can be drawn from another media accountability system, that of the Broadcasting Complaints Commission of South Africa (BCCSA). Established by the National Association of Broadcasters in 1993, the BCCSA is responsible for accepting and adjudicating complaints against the content of the broadcast media of radio and television. The first principles of the 'BCCSA Free-to-Air Code of Conduct for Broadcasting Service Licensees' (BCCSA 2009: 7) read as follows:

11 News

(1) Broadcasting service licensees must report news truthfully, accurately and fairly.

(2) News must be presented in the correct context and in a fair manner, without intentional or negligent departure from the facts, whether by:

    (a)   Distortion, exaggeration or misrepresentation;

    (b)   Material omissions; or

    (c)   Summarisation.

(3) Only that which may reasonably be true, having reasonable regard to the source of the news, may be presented as fact, and such fact must be broadcast fairly with reasonable regard to context and importance.

When remembering the importance of voice(s), and when recognising the ethics of listening as an enabler of human dignity, these first principles become crucial. However, it is their implementation by our media accountability mechanisms that casts a degree of hypocrisy on both these codes, as well as the journalistic reporting that is subject to the standard of ethics required therein.

For example, according to the above, we expect print and digital news media journalists to present news 'in context and in a balanced manner' (PCSA 2016: clause 1.2). With regard to the ethical requirement of balance: very simply, how can a news story be considered to contain 'balance' when it does not contain the views, perspectives, narratives or voice(s) of the people most directly impacted by the events or conditions on which the news content reports? As mentioned earlier in this book, and as demonstrated evidentially in the preceding chapters, mainstream news media reporting tends to source the perspectives of officialdom, while most often overlooking the voice(s) of the marginalised and poor, who are frequently positioned at the very centre of events but whose voice(s) are not regarded as important enough for inclusion in reportage. Here, the voices of officialdom and of the elites dominate the public sphere and news reporting. People on the ground, who are directly impacted by the events to which reportage refers, are seldom heard. Clearly, only the proverbial one side of the story makes it into the news. Can we really call this kind of journalism 'balanced'? Equally, can we call it 'truthful', 'accurate' or 'fair', as is demanded in the first principles of both codes of ethics above?

We heard regular accounts from the people we interviewed in the three communities we visited of instances where journalistic reporting had simply got the facts wrong regarding events that had taken place. Without engaging the ethics of listening, and by ignoring the voice(s) of the community members of Glebelands, Thembelihle and Xolobeni, journalists failed to talk to the people who were eyewitnesses to events, who could give first-hand accounts of what happened, and who could narrate detailed histories of the conflicts and struggles related to events in each site, thus providing the 'context' required by both of these codes of ethics. Journalists got the facts wrong because they neglected to talk to the people who were there when things happened.

Truthfulness, accuracy, fairness and balance are idealistically considered crucial components of journalistic credibility. But, in light of all of the above, can a news story be legitimately credible when it fails to include the voice(s) of people at the grassroots, when the news story bears direct relevance to their lives? The answer is no. Our media accountability systems and regulatory bodies need to take heed of the ethics of listening just as acutely as practising news journalists and media outlets. These accountability systems must revise their own understanding of the first principles, and naturally revise existing codes of ethics accordingly to insert and forefront the aspect of voice(s).

For example, a press council ought to consider it unacceptable when a news story reports on the prospecting interests of a foreign company and their intentions to establish a new mine on our shores, without also including the perspectives of the people who reside in the region and whose lives have been or stand to be indelibly altered by the actions and decisions of both the foreign company as well as national and local state actors. Of course, it is in the interests of such corporate capital and political elites that journalism tends to function as it does, because it gives this 'officialdom' a monopoly on the narrative within the public sphere. That is, when journalists only consult these 'official' sources, the official sources say only what they wish the public to hear. They do not even necessarily need to lie, but only provide information that would be considered palatable.

It is often only when interacting with the grassroots that one learns of the unpalatable things that have happened, such as acts of violence, intimidation, bribery, corruption, or the reality of the manner in which the local community's lived conditions have been or will be impacted by events. While we addressed the political economy of dominant power and storytelling in chapter 7, the first principles of ethics and the credibility of the journalistic profession is also at stake. By neglecting grassroots voice(s), crucial facts are often missed and not reported. The supposed truth, accuracy, fairness and balance we demand of our journalism then becomes a myth, imbued with hypocrisy.

Media accountability mechanisms, codes of journalistic ethics and conduct, and media best-practice standards profess the importance of fairness, balance and accuracy in investigative reporting. However, these bodies, codes and standards largely ignore the negative impact of the exclusion of voice(s) on these principles. But this needs to change. It would not take much effort to revise the codes of ethics and complaints procedures of our media accountability mechanisms to include regulatory clauses that specifically address the representation of voice(s), in the interest of fairness, balance, truthfulness and accuracy in news media reporting.

Revising the understanding and related definitions of the first principles on paper in the codes of ethics is a first and important step. But the revision of the institutional nature and structure of the media accountability bodies, which are responsible for adjudicating according to these codes, is equally important, most especially with regard to their accessibility. Some will argue that communities who feel aggrieved towards the news media, where a particular report lacks balance, have the right of redress through the already established media accountability mechanisms. Can such a community approach the relevant regulator and lay a complaint? Yes. But, unfortunately, it is not that simple. Most often, these regulatory mechanisms are simply out of the reach of ordinary people, particularly poor and marginalised communities. What follows below is a story that serves as an example of the inaccessibility of media accountability mechanisms.

The story of the Glebelands Hostel Community Violence Victims (GHCVV) and the since dissolved television news broadcaster, African News Network 7 (ANN7), serves as a pertinent and poignant demonstration of how media accountability systems are simply out of reach for many ordinary people. In this case, the complainants or the persons negatively impacted by a news story were from an extremely vulnerable, poor and marginalised community, some of whom had their personal safety put at risk due to the content of a news broadcast.

To appreciate the seriousness of the breach of ethics committed by the broadcaster, this case must be understood within its socio-political context. As mentioned in preceding chapters, the Glebelands hostel community has for many years been beset by violence, which has significantly increased in intensity since 2014. An estimated 160 people have been assassinated in Glebelands since March 2014, with an average of two to three murders occurring within this close-knit community per month (Right2Know Campaign 2015; Sefali 2015). When Dale McKinley and I visited Glebelands, some community members organised a group of local men to act as armed guards for us. They kept watch, spread out and formed a perimeter around the spot where we held our meeting and interviews, all of which took place in an old rickety carport constructed out of corrugated iron. This structure was riddled with bullet holes. From beneath the structure, I could look out towards the nearest hostel building. A second-floor window was broken. A few weeks before, violent thugs had broken into the room with the broken window, killed a man, and thrown his body out of the window. The man's 14-year-old son had been in the room at the time.

Many community members have been traumatised by the ongoing violence, which is not limited to murder but includes the endemic rape of women, illegal evictions and torture at the hands of criminals. Reportedly much violence is also either performed by South African Police Service (SAPS) officials, or at least enabled by SAPS inaction to prevent it. The socio-political conditions surrounding Glebelands and the causes of the violence are multifarious and complex, but, in brief, they involve the often intertwining interests of colluding criminal warlords, including taxi transport operators, allegedly corrupt police officials, and politically motivated violence spurred on by local government municipal ward councillors and hired assassins. Some among the 160 people from the community who have been murdered include whistle-blowers scheduled to give testimony against the police services and/or police officials.

The Glebelands community is acutely economically marginalised and disenabled. Residents are often prevented from seeking employment: their movements within the area of the hostel compound are severely restricted by violent criminals, making it unsafe to travel to and from their place of employment. The hostels are surrounded by 'no-go zones': anyone crossing these zones runs the risk of being shot by criminals who stand guard. Whistle-blowers have also provided information on the existence of several hit lists, which contain the names of individuals who are scheduled to be killed by varying factions within the highly charged environment. The killings are most often not random, but, indeed, targeted and organised.

A group of concerned people from the community, the aforementioned GHCVV, appealed to various authorities, both locally and nationally, for official action that could stem the tide of violence. They followed all official procedures and avenues available to them, including seeking assistance from SAPS management, the South African Public Protector, the South African parliament and various bodies of state. All efforts of this nature had, by April 2015, proved ineffectual. In an act of desperation and as a final effort to receive assistance from any official body, the GHCVV issued a request for intervention to the United Nations Human

Rights Council, and summarily held a press conference to publically announce their request that the United Nations intervene to ensure that the South African government act to bring a halt to the killings and violence within the stricken community (Madlala 2016). Unfortunately, it was this press conference that set in motion a media ethics breach of the severest kind, resulting in further risk to the personal safety of a number of Glebelands community members.

The press conference was held on Sunday, 17 April 2016 at the Glebelands hostel compound. Prior to the press conference, both a press release and an invitation to the media were circulated electronically, and both of these communiqués to the media contained the following portion of text: 'NB: Due to serious security concerns we ask all attendees to refrain from identifying individual members of the community unless specific permission is obtained from the person concerned' (Glebelands Hostel Community Violence Victims 2016a, 2016b). In addition, on arrival at the press conference all members of the media present were briefed by representatives of the GHCVV and instructed that they should not under any circumstances reveal the identities of any of the individual community members (either by naming, publishing photographs or broadcasting images of them in a manner that could result in them being identified). Members of the press were urged to pixelate the faces and distort the voices of the GHCVV who would be addressing the press conference. The GHCVV took these measures as a result of fear that they would be targeted by criminals and potentially by SAPS officials for speaking to the media or bringing public attention to the dire situation in Glebelands, and for emphasising the impunity enjoyed by criminals and murderers.

Given the socio-political context of the Glebelands community, their fears were well founded. The press conference took place the day after the murder of an African National Congress (ANC) proportional representation councillor, Zodwa Sibiya, also a Glebelands hostel resident (Savides 2016). So, while people from the Glebelands community fear for their lives daily, the GHCVV members who addressed the media at the press conference performed a brave act. While warning the journalists present of the dangers they faced to their personal safety, they put their confidence in the media and thereafter entrusted the media with their lives.

The day after the press conference, ANN7 subsequently broadcast footage of the press conference held at the Glebelands hostel compound at regular intervals throughout the day, but without having taken any of the measures requested to conceal the faces or voices of those present. The personal identities of many of the members of the GHCVV were clearly identifiable in the broadcast footage. The same footage was also published as an online video on the ANN7 website, where, again, no attempt was made to conceal the personal identities of the community members. The GHCVV then contacted the ANN7 reporter who attended the press conference. Shortly thereafter, both the reporter and the ANN7 assignment editor apologised to the GHCVV and informed them that the originally broadcast footage of the GHCVV press conference would be removed from the ANN7 website, and would no longer be broadcast on the ANN7 television news channel. The content was summarily removed from both platforms.

However, shortly thereafter, ANN7 began broadcasting an in-studio interview with a South African National Civic Organisation representative, Toenka Matila, on the topic of Glebelands hostel violence. During the interview, stock footage of the very same press conference was again aired, and the personal identities of the GHCVV who attended were again revealed on air, for a second time. The Matila interview was published in its entirety as an online video on the ANN7 website, and remained on the website for two days. Moreover, the Matila interview was also published as aggregated content on the website of *The New Age* newspaper, *New Age Online* (both this newspaper and news website have since closed down).

After the initial broadcast that revealed the GHCVV members' identities, ANN7 offered the GHCVV assurances that the oversight had been corrected by the broadcaster. Evidently, this was not the case, since within a day the same footage was rebroadcast on television, republished online and also republished on the website of another news outlet (*New Age Online*) as part of the Matila interview. On 21 April 2016, the GHCVV contacted ANN7 for a second time, and again requested that the content be removed from all of its news platforms. The broadcaster obliged. Nonetheless, by this point the footage that revealed the personal identities of the GHCVV had already been in the public domain and was freely available on both the ANN7 website as well as the *New Age Online* website for a full three days.

Once the initial task of convincing the broadcaster to desist from revealing the personal identities of the GHCVV in the public domain had been concluded, the GHCVV decided to lodge a complaint against ANN7 with the appropriate regulatory body, the BCCSA. On the surface of it, the seriousness of the case became immediately evident. This should be understood in relative terms to other complaints administered by the BCCSA or the PCSA, where the majority of these involve questions of fairness and/or accuracy, balance, dignity, or instances in which the complainant was not afforded reasonable time or the opportunity to comment and/or the right of reply (Reid and Isaacs 2015). Rarely does a complaint involve content that has the potential to catalyse violence and physical harm. But in this particular case, the offending news content held this potential, and the complainants' lives were subsequently put at risk. The seriousness of the complaint was further compounded because the broadcaster had committed the breach twice.

The serious nature of the case meant that laying a complaint with the relevant media regulatory body, in this case the BCCSA, was indeed appropriate. However, at this point the *Glebelands v ANN7* case surfaced problematic barriers of accessibility to the BCCSA system. Throughout the process of the administration of the complaint by the BCCSA in the case, it became clear that the complaint would likely have never reached conclusion were it not for the voluntary interventions of well-resourced individuals acting as representatives for the GHCVV.

I am an academic specialising in the study of media regulation and policy, and I am full-time employed by a university. Justine Limpitlaw is a widely renowned media lawyer and has authored various titles on media law and regulation. Both of us immediately volunteered to act as representatives for the GHCVV in respect of their BCCSA complaint on a pro bono basis. In doing so, we took on the responsibility of compiling, writing and submitting the complaint, as well as the associated administrative tasks, and we represented the GHCVV at the subsequent BCCSA tribunal hearing in Johannesburg.

The Glebelands hostel community is one of extreme poverty, where many people are unemployed. Most of the residents do not have access to the communications mechanisms (email or telephones), which are required to lay a complaint with the BCCSA, and to respond to correspondence received from the BCCSA throughout the complaints process (of which there was a great deal). The processes of the BCCSA, its procedural documents, including its constitution and complaints procedure, are conducted and published in English. None of the Glebelands residents practise English as their first language. No provision was made by the BCCSA to address the Glebelands residents in their language of preference.

In addition, the BCCSA's procedural documents would be difficult for a person to understand if he/she is not familiar with media regulatory terminology, which cannot be expected of most ordinary South African citizens, whether they are economically marginalised or not. Resultantly, Justine and I, together with community liaison Vanessa Burger, had to engage, consult and guide the complainants in this case through each step of the lengthy process in order to make sure that the relevant community members correctly understood each aspect of the administration of the complaint. While we were glad to do so, this ought not to have been our responsibility, but that of the BCCSA itself. In the absence of our voluntary assistance to this community, the BCCSA had no measures in place to assist these complainants throughout the complicated regulatory process.

At one point during the administration of the complaint, the BCCSA required all affected persons from the Glebelands community to sign a waiver document before the administration of the complaint could proceed. Given the context of the Glebelands hostels, this seemingly simple task was extremely difficult to accomplish. First, none of the GHCVV has access to a computer or printer. Since both Justine and I are based in Gauteng and not Durban, we then had to provide funds to the GHCVV for travel and communications purposes, so that one of them could travel into central Durban to an internet café, download the waiver document, and print a number of hard copies of the document. This individual then had to meet with the relevant community members in Glebelands, and collect the signed waiver documents at a later date. Thereafter, she had to travel back to the internet café, scan the signed documents and email these back to us at an additional cost.

Firstly, all of this put the individual who performed this task at great personal risk since she had to move about the hostel compound to meet with the relevant community members, as well as travelling to the internet café. Secondly, the cost of accessing the relevant communications mechanisms in order to administer the waiver documents required by the BCCSA was simply out of reach for this poor community.

The pro bono voluntary involvement of persons with high levels of expertise in media policy and regulation on the part of the complainant in this case should be noted as an exception. The procedural structure of the BCCSA does not make provision for complainants who would require assistance in accessing or participating in the regulatory system. By comparison, the PCSA appoints a public advocate for this very purpose. Section 6.5 of the constitution of the PCSA outlines the appointment and duties of the public advocate and includes that the position requires having a finely tuned sense of public service and commitment. The public advocate assists members of the public in formulating complaints, may attempt to resolve complaints amicably by mediating settlements, or, if the complaint proceeds to a hearing, may also act as the complainant's representative before the ombudsman and/or the appeals panel.

The latter is a key factor. In the Glebelands case, Justine and I represented the complainants at the BCCSA tribunal, which was held in Johannesburg. Had we not done so, the complainant would have had no representation at the tribunal hearing whatsoever. Even if the concerned

Glebelands community members had somehow managed to administer the complaints process on their own until it reached the tribunal phase, none of these people would have had the financial capability to travel from Durban to Johannesburg in order to attend the tribunal. The forum of the tribunal would then have been heavily weighted against the complainant and in favour of the broadcaster, since the complainant would not have been able to present the GHCVV case to the BCCSA chairperson and panel.

The environmental and economic conditions of the Glebelands hostel community are by no means unique within South Africa, where poverty and inequality are key descriptors of the daily life of the majority of people. The high cost of telecommunications and data services in South Africa, relative to other countries, means that the majority do not enjoy meaningful access to these communicative services, including the internet (Abrahams and Pillay 2014). Additionally, language barriers persist, where the predominant language of conducting business in state institutions, as well as media regulatory systems, is English. South Africa is a country where the largest majority are not first-language English speakers, a reality that privileges those who have a good grasp of the English language.

Given these multifarious contextual factors, the process of administering a complaint from an economically disadvantaged individual or community (who are the majority) with the BCCSA evidently privileges broadcasters to a significant extent, since broadcasters do not suffer a lack of resources and capacity to the same degree as, for example, a poor grassroots community. The process itself is therefore weighted in favour of broadcasters and against poor and marginalised peoples, both in economic terms, as well as with regard to having access to those with the expertise to take part and act as representatives in the BCCSA complaints process. While it may be beyond the powers of media regulatory institutions to lessen these difficult environmental factors, it is in the public interest to become sensitive to them. While the accessibility and ease of use of the PCSA system has been significantly improved through the appointment of the public advocate, the same cannot be said of the BCCSA.

This is of additional concern because it involves the regulatory body for broadcasters. As a media type, broadcasting, and particularly the public service of the SABC, enjoys a pseudo monopoly over audience numbers. Various factors involving barriers to media access for the poor means that media consumption of news content via print newspapers or the internet among this segment of the population is low. The low-cost nature of free-to-air broadcasting, particularly radio, means that this media type features most prominently in the media repertoires of the majority of the South African audience (Duncan and Reid 2013). Resultantly, the media type (broadcasting) that has by far the largest audience numbers and the greatest monopoly over the media landscape with regard to content also has the weakest degree of accessibility for the largest segment of the population.

Despite all of the above, the eventual outcome of the *Glebelands v ANN7* case was marginally positive for the Glebelands community. After a tribunal hearing, the BCCSA chairperson found that the broadcaster had committed gross negligence, and ordered ANN7 to broadcast a public apology admitting the errant conduct (Viljoen 2016). ANN7 summarily obliged. This outcome certainly provided some vindication to the Glebelands community members who were negatively impacted by the broadcast. After ANN7 broadcast its public apology, the GHCVV released a press statement, in which they expressly called for the appointment of a public advocate at the BCCSA, given their experience of participation in the regulatory system, which was characterised by its inaccessibility (Glebelands Hostel Community Violence Victims 2016c). To date, this recommendation has not yet been enacted by the BCCSA.

Asking that our media accountability systems ought to be more sensitive to the real and lived conditions of ordinary people is not unreasonable. It is not a big ask, for example, that these bodies should publish their codes of ethics and complaints procedures in all of the country's official languages. While the PCSA can at least be applauded for the institution of the office of the public advocate, both of these bodies need to take more heed of the circumstances of the majority of ordinary people and communities. The difficulty in accessing digital communications media and something as seemingly simple as email, as was the case for the Glebelands community, is but one example. South African communities who have grievances with news media content, as many of them do, should not have to rely solely on the intervention of a pair of well-resourced 'experts' in order for their voice(s) to be taken seriously within media accountability systems.

As much as professional journalists need to pay more attention to the respectful interaction with voice(s) and practice, and ethics of listening, so too must the media accountability institutions that profess to uphold the codes of ethics to which journalists are held to account.

10

Planting the Seeds of Change

Julie Reid

> Honest reporters approach every situation with humility: they find the people
> who don't get listened to and really listen to them. They get to know a place.
> — Katharine Viner, editor-in-chief of *The Guardian*

A n enriched and augmented understanding of voice(s), and a more broadly active practice of listening, particularly with respect to marginalised voices, is not only a necessary moral obligation on the part of the news media but also one that stands to positively benefit the media sector itself, as well as the socio-political space. Chapter 8 addressed how inclusive media diversity, which works as a simple but important model for the active inclusion of voice(s), would not only encourage higher levels of media content diversity available to media audiences, but would also go some way to bolstering the financial sustainability of large portions of the news media sector, while also adding to the news media's all-important credibility.

But the broader inclusion of voice(s) in the mainstream news media sphere would do more than benefit the media sector alone. As previously discussed, particularly in the first chapter, the practice of listening journalism and the insertion of previously ignored voice(s) into the mainstream information landscape would provide greater opportunity for social cohesion, for problem solving and for a better informed citizenry, which could then possess a much more complete sketch of what is actually happening in the world. The collective conversations of societies are unlikely to arrive at solutions to the problems of our time when so many of us are able to see so small a portion of the whole picture. Inclusive media diversity, then, is about trying to make the world a better place.

LISTENING RESEARCH

Where are we at present with regard to making this happen? Firstly, within the news media sector a small collection of commendable media outlets, some of which have been mentioned in this book, assume the primacy of grassroots and marginalised voice(s) as central to the way they make news. But these are considerably limited in number and appear mostly as independent or community media outlets. Public service media and corporatised private media have yet to follow suit in any significant way. While these dominant media types still draw the bulk of audience figures, the largest majority of news media consumers are then exposed to crucially low levels of inclusive media diversity in their information diets.

Secondly, and with regard to research and teaching, a small but steadily growing number of researchers have in recent years given attention to both the dominant media's disproportionate representation of narratives relevant to small segments of the citizenry, as well as the theorisation of voice and the notion of listening as central to the process of the inclusion of voice(s).[1] However, research needs to be expanded beyond this observable dominant media behaviour and theoretical positions in order to encompass formulations of the practical application of inclusive media diversity, the inclusion of voice(s) and the practice of listening journalism. For academic researchers, the task is twofold. First is the necessity to find out 'the how': how can the news media practically engage inclusive media diversity? Second is the task of teaching: how do we train our current scholars and future newsmakers on how to be listening journalists?

But where academics must teach future journalists a respect for voice(s) and the practical yet meaningful engagement in the process of listening, they cannot effectively do this if they are not aware of how to achieve it themselves. Listening research will by necessity need to precede the teaching of listening journalism. Unfortunately, the present and predominant structural architecture of the global higher education system provides a foundationally unfertile environment for the task.

Research traditions institutionalised within research practices developed in the global North bear symmetry with a capitalist worldview in their emphasis on individualism. This is obvious in the very structure of the academic system. Take, for example, academic journal publications: academics generally receive more credit for single-authored articles than co-authored ones. Here, not only is collaborative or collective research literally discouraged by the economic imperatives of the university and the academic publishing system itself, but sharing 'authorship' with a group or community of grassroots peoples, none of whom are likely to be academic professionals themselves, becomes unthinkable. The dominant individualist paradigm of the higher education system weighs heavily against the collectivist necessity of listening research.

In many scenarios, career advancement for academics depends mostly on publications, which both encourages individualism and creates a 'bean-counting' culture, in which the number of publications symptomatically takes precedence over the value of the research performed in terms of its impact and potential to initiate positive social change. This is one way in which critical thought and in-depth empirical research suffers. The architecture of this environment also supports the academic journal publishing industry: where academics are very much aware that their own job security rests on publishing as much as possible (regardless of the quality thereof), profiteering academic journals benefit immensely.

But the entire industry is one that is decidedly unjust, from the exploitative treatment of the academics to the closed-door, non-availability of the published research, locked away behind expensive paywalls and unavailable to the public, even where public funds have been used to finance the research. This is at odds with the democratic ideal of the social sciences. Where it is the purpose of the social sciences to explore solutions to societal problems, the presentation of such 'solutions' cannot benefit a society when no one is able to read about them.

The situation, however, is not static and pushbacks are surfacing. Various movements, such as Access2Research and the Public Knowledge Project, have opposed the closed-access journal publishing model. The pirate website Sci-Hub uses a crowd-sourcing model to make scientific literature, originally published in subscription journals, freely available and open source to anyone wishing to read them. Sci-Hub currently hosts an estimated 81.6 million scholarly articles. A recent study by bio-data scientists at the University of Pennsylvania concluded that Sci-Hub provides access to 85.2 per cent of articles published in closed-access journals, and is able to provide access for 99.3 per cent of incoming requests.

As explained by Daniel Himmelstein et al. (2017): 'Hence, the scope of this resource suggests the subscription publishing model is becoming unsustainable. For the first time, the overwhelming majority of scholarly literature is available gratis to anyone with an Internet connection.' Perhaps there is hope. Still, universities all over the world are increasingly market-driven, which has been extremely harmful to students, to the promotion of lateral critical thinking and to research and inquiry – all of which are the ideals towards which higher education ought to strive (Sage and Polychroniou 2016).

The social sciences, most especially the communications sciences such as media studies, marketing, public relations and journalism, are crucial to the survival of dominant power in its neo-liberal capitalist incarnation because these are mechanisms required for the systematic reiteration of the dominant mythologies and narratives that naturalise the position of the elite. Herein lies a conundrum for dominant power: while the social sciences are key to its survival, they also provide platforms for the kind of lateral critical thinking that could initiate its demise. The most powerful arsenal that dominant capital power has at its disposal, money, is manipulated to deal with this problem. Having monetised almost every sphere of human life, funding for the social sciences is also manoeuvred according to the needs of dominant capital.

Research in information technologies, for example, is well funded, while funding for social scientific pursuits, which could potentially promote more critical modes of thought and/or develop alternatives to the capitalist economic organisation of society, such as philosophy, are woefully underfunded. The corporatist embodiment of capitalism at universities means that any discipline that entertains the potential to expose, critique and formulate alternatives to the system, which is destroying the planetary ecology while simultaneously sustaining and increasing the unequal organisation of humanity, is described as being an unnecessary drain on the university's finances, not viable due to a lack of attracting student numbers and therefore generally not viable at all (Olivier 2016).

The likelihood then of attaining the necessary funding for the desperately needed research endeavours, which would seek to investigate practical ways of amplifying the voice(s) of poor and marginalised people within national debates and the public sphere, is not very high. This is because it is these voice(s) that can most acutely expose the failings of the current dominant organisation of human society, and it is therefore these voices that must be kept quiet, or more accurately, remain under-represented.

Academics face another reality of listening research, which is out of synch with the architecture of the higher education system: listening research takes time, and a lot of it. Similar to listening journalism, listening research requires processes of meaningful listening, preceded by a period of relationship-building within a particular community or group of people. Such processes cannot and should not be rushed. The tough ask for academic researchers in the social sciences today is to perform this kind of research work with little funding, knowing that they are likely to attain limited personal individualised acclaim and sacrifice career advancement to some degree by putting primary focus on high-quality and slow-to-produce research, rather than high-quantity, speedy publishing.

Clearly, the dominant structural architecture of the higher education sector requires serious overhaul if the environment is to become more fertile ground for the fostering of the social scientific ideal. In the coming years, one can hope that the now global decolonisation project will include within its ambit not just the transformation of university curricula and the reduction in costs to the student for access to higher education but also a dismantling and reformation of the currently unjust structure of the dominant university system.

THE LISTENING JOURNALIST

Securing the advancement of inclusive media diversity requires major paradigm shifts within the journalistic profession and dominant media sphere, as much as it does within the higher education sector. We intentionally wrote this book as a demonstration of purposeful listening in order to surface voice(s) and stories from the ground, in the hopes that it would function as an example to working and aspirant journalists of how this can be done (see chapters 2–5). When confronted with the low levels of coverage of community and grassroots voice(s) within the dominant media, as evidenced in chapter 6, journalists and editors may likely offer the retort of a lack of funding for serious journalistic work. It is true that the news media sector is under strain with regard to its financial sustainability, and the resources allocated to newsrooms are often too tight. Nonetheless, there remain avenues to follow that would positively increase inclusive media diversity through journalistic listening that do not cost any money.

Firstly, a change of attitude: little empirical research has been performed on the perceptions of journalists towards their audience or to marginalised persons, relative to other areas of media research (Ngomba 2011). However, in 2017, Anthea Garman and Vanessa Malila (2017) did just that, investigating the attitudes of a sample of South African journalists and editors with regard to a meaningful understanding of listening, and also interrogated their understandings of their own role in South Africa, particularly in relation to young people who are finding their political voice. The findings of their study are not encouraging.

The research showed that listening as a journalistic practice is seldom understood in anything more than common-sense ways and is certainly not an organising principle of reporting and disseminating news. This results in journalism that is events-focused, often sensationalist and the agenda of which is set powerfully and predominantly by political actions and actors in the environment. Here, the possibility of being heard rests solely in the hands of the journalists, who, while they may regard themselves as 'the voice of the people', do little to actively engage with the grassroots or provide a space for active listening to the voice(s) of community members (Garman and Malila 2017: 1). While this field of inquiry requires further investigation, the results of this study suggest that an adjustment of attitude among journalists and editors is required, one that emphasises a consciousness of their role as listeners. So, a first step towards promoting inclusive media diversity is for journalists themselves to engage in a little introspection and shift their own attitudes with regard to not only reporting on but also listening to people who may be poor and marginalised but are directly impacted by the events that are the subject of a news story.

Secondly, journalists need to understand the very nature of their own profession differently. The promotion of genuine listening journalism does not just mean a change of attitude, but a paradigm shift regarding the journalistic profession. In South Africa, the consequences of a post-1994 era of often politically motivated dubious dealings, rampant corruption and government mismanagement have had two key impacts on media behaviour. First, the mainstream news media's primary focus has too often been directed solely at probing the political elite and high-level power structures – the very top of the societal pyramid – while having little time to focus on what is happening to the lower, yet much larger portions, of that same pyramid. Second, due largely to this and also compounded by the situation of a weak institutional political opposition and one-party dominance, the news media has indulged in a watchdog role and inadvertently assumed the purpose of the real opposition (Satgar 2010). The mythologisation of the news media's watchdog role has subsequently become deeply entrenched in South African mainstream journalism. That does not mean that the watchdog role is not important and necessary, but only that it is not enough, and it is not the only role for journalists to play. Apart from performing as the watchdog, journalists and editors ought to equally become members of the pack.

The metaphor of the transformation of the journalist from 'watchdog' to a 'member of the pack' connotes a deeper connectedness with the public or society (the pack), which the news sector purports to serve. This pack-member metaphor ought not to be confused with 'pack journalism' as described by Jane Duncan (2012) in her media content analysis of the news coverage of Marikana, and discussed in chapter 1, which is the type of journalism that leads to reduced diversity, sameness and, crucially, inaccurate accounting of the facts. Further, the pack-member role need not be understood as being at odds with the watchdog role, but rather as complementary to it. The watchdog journalist, committed to probing the upper echelons and exposing, for example, government failings or mismanagement, need only recognise that stories emanating from grassroots level are often the most acutely hard-hitting demonstrations of how a government has failed its people. The pack-member journalist knows the value of marginalised voice(s) in that they offer counter-narratives to those of dominant power, often revealing how the decisions and actions of powerful political elites at the top of the pyramid can have disastrous consequences for ordinary people and communities on the ground. Listening is the natural accompaniment to such voice(s). Voice cannot have effect, cannot be successful and cannot matter without listening. For journalists to master listening, they need to be more deeply involved with voice(s) from the ground, that is, become a metaphorical pack member as opposed to performing a solely watchdog role.

The pack-member role is not one that simply relegates journalists to acting as conduits for citizens' voice(s) from the grassroots into the mediated sphere. Instead, journalists facilitate the connection of horizontal discussions from the ground up and along the vertical axis of political power. The news media has the ability to inculcate national or global discussions with the voice(s) that are best placed to speak to the struggles of ordinary people. Herman Wasserman (2013: 79) expands on this role thus:

> The difference is that the agenda for these questions will not be set only by journalists themselves, but also by citizens – and not only in the fashionable 'citizen journalism' of 'user-generated content' on newspaper websites that does little to shift the dominant journalistic paradigm. Listening as an ethical imperative for journalists is a much more radical project. It entails a subversion of the very foundational assumptions about journalists as 'gatekeepers', by turning them into 'gateopeners' who decentralise the power structure inherent in media production and involve news subjects as equal partners in the production process.

Thirdly, journalists must relinquish their sense of sole authorship of a story. Listening journalism requires that journalists abandon their desire to personally determine the contents of the reported narrative, but rather engage in a collaborative authorship, allowing for the inclusion of the voice(s) of people to whom the story has relevance, and to whom the story may make a difference. This becomes a subversion of the individualist paradigm of both academia as well as the mode of Northern/Western-style journalism, which we have inherited, appropriated and maintained in South Africa. Listening journalism abandons individual authorship in the traditional sense and engages a more participatory mode of story production, where the agenda is not only set by the journalist, but includes the input of the people, citizens and the community who are at the centre of the story. The pack-member journalist is guided by their directives, desires, interests and voice(s), and storytelling then becomes a collective and participatory project. In chapter 2 we outlined, for example, what this means for one of the most fundamental tasks of journalistic work: interviewing. The journalist's role here changes from that of the 'expert' gatherer of 'relevant' information, armed with a predetermined set of rigid questions, to that of the active listener who allows lateral space for the narration of diverse voice(s). In this scenario, the journalist is not the expert, but instead recognises that the real 'experts' on the story are those who have actually lived through its events, and felt its impacts on their daily lives.

Fourthly, journalists ought to seek a better and broader understanding of the fundamental principles of good reporting. In chapter 9 we explained that the fundamental first principles of ethical journalism require that it be reasonably true, fair, accurate and balanced. However, a news story that predominantly foregrounds the voices of officialdom and offers little to no representation of the views, perspectives, narratives or voice(s) of the people most directly impacted by the conditions on which the news content reports, cannot be considered 'balanced' reporting. It is one-sided. Equally, the truthfulness and accuracy of any news report is likely to be undermined when journalists do not follow a basic foundational principle of reporting, that is, talk (and listen) to the people who were actually there and who saw first-hand what happened. Remembering how the dominant media initially misrepresented the true nature of events subsequent to the Marikana massacre (described in chapter 1), we also heard from the communities that we worked with of instances where the news media had simply got the facts wrong because journalists neglected to talk with people who were first-hand witnesses to events (see chapter 9). When journalists neglect to talk to the people who were on the scene when things happened, important information is missed, and facts are often wrong. And any journalist who values their own professional credibility should be loath to get the facts wrong.

Here, journalists can enact the three-step formula for inclusive media diversity that we offered in chapter 8. Step one involves identifying the voices and perspectives that are already or routinely listened to and represented on any particular issue or news narrative. Step two means looking for, listening out for and actively listening to the voice(s) of the unheard or under-represented. Step three is the product of a participatory process of listening and engagement with the voice(s) identified in step two – the dignified inclusion of these voices in news reporting.

Fifthly, journalists must master the art of listening. Journalists must again practice introspection, this time with regard to their own class positions. The personal discomfort associated with engaging voice(s) from contexts and situations that bear little symmetry with one's own should be openly acknowledged and confronted. Making the news through listening journalism means that journalists need to step outside of their own comfort zones. This is not always an easy thing to do, but it is also not impossible to learn, practice and, in time, grow comfortable with. Indeed, if one is not willing to really listen to people who are not like oneself, then why become a journalist at all?

Deep listening means that the pack-member journalist seeks not only those sound-bite clips that appear to have a direct relevance to the issue at hand, but rather rich histories, a broader understanding of the context and interrelated but possibly varying accounts. The dominant news media function principally as an event-orientated medium, reporting events as they take place but failing to join the dots and explain recent developments within the context of a continuing narrative, thus foregoing the opportunity for audiences to understand current events properly. We noted this habitual characteristic in dominant news media coverage in our media content analysis explained in chapter 6. The pack-member journalist must endeavour to break this dominant mould and surface voice(s) within their associated context, history and as part of an ongoing narrative rather than as an isolated and insular event.

As evidenced by our media content analysis as well as by many other research studies, the dominant media regularly attributes more importance to voices of authority and officialdom. The pack-member journalist, however, ought to always consider these 'official' voices with a healthy degree of scepticism, recognising that a local politician, a minister, a representative of the police services or the spokesperson of a corporate entity are all motivated in their speech by their particular version of events, which is driven by political and/or economic imperatives. The voice of officialdom is seldom innocently lacking in veiled but particular motivations, and the pack-member journalist ought never to assume that a full or complete picture of events is wholly explicated by official sources.

Apart from recognising that official voices are seldom innocent, the pack-member journalist should treat the voice(s) of the marginalised, the poor and of grassroots communities with an equitable degree of importance as voices of authority. This is because, when in search of the truth, the significance of facts ought to be determined by whether they are indeed true and not by a social hierarchy that delegates degrees of truthfulness or importance, depending on where their source is situated in that social hierarchy.

Finally, key to mastering the art of listening is learning how to let people tell their own story. It is remembering that the people who have lived through a particular set of events know things and have borne witness to things, which, as an 'outsider', the journalist does not know, has not seen and has not even thought to look for. These details, nuances, histories and crucial facts can only be surfaced and discovered through engaged listening.

In chapter 2 we described our own strategy for conducting interviews: we did not approach the interview with a stringent predetermined set of must-ask questions. Doing so would have superficially led the participants to speak only to the aspects of the story that we already knew about. Instead, we did not ask the people we talked with to focus on any particular aspect, event or key category as identified by us. We only asked them to tell their story. When we did so we heard about aspects relevant to each community, about which we knew nothing before we got there, and about which we would have learned nothing had we tried to force the interviewee to speak to a list of specific questions. Listening journalism requires relinquishing authority of the storytelling moment, and giving command of this interaction to the person to whom it rightly belongs – the storyteller.

* * *

IN CLOSING

For Nick Couldry (2009: 579–580):

> Listening here is, first and foremost, the act of recognizing what others have to say, recognizing that they have something to say or, better, that they, like all human beings, have the capacity to give an account of their lives that is reflexive and continuous, an ongoing, embodied process of reflection … The reason we need to listen – and the reason why, arguably, depending on how we want to frame things, we have an 'obligation' to listen – is that all human beings have the capacity for voice, to give an account of their lives.

The change required here lies in transforming the news media from an event-orientated to a story-orientated medium.

Giving meaningful space to voice(s) means that many different actors need to come to the table. The task requires the cooperation of media owners, news editors and journalists. Additionally, it requires a rethink of the structural impediments within the university system described here, which act as stumbling blocks to performing necessary further research but also the subsequent training of our future newsmakers. Equally, theoretical paradigm shifts and a process of redefining the very terminology that we collectively adopt in media theory, media politics and regulation are necessary. Chapter 9 addresses how and why this is crucial regarding the concepts of media freedom and, in terms of journalistic ethics, the notions of balance, accuracy and fairness. But this is far from an exclusive list of terms and concepts that for decades we have treated as immutable, but which, when viewed through a decolonised lens with an audience-centred perspective, demand serious revision. There are many more fundamental, basic, normative and now overly naturalised terms, concepts, theories and regulatory practices that require discussion, revision and research in order to make them more symmetrical with audience-centredness and more inclusionary in nature.

Further, the exclusionary character of some of our media accountability mechanisms is evident not only in how grassroots citizens are disenabled from gaining access to these, but also within the operational documents of these institutions and in the very codes of ethics that are meant to be used as a yardstick to guide ethical journalistic behaviour. Similar inquiries could justifiably be made into the exclusionary character of the editorial guideline documents adopted as internal regulations by large media corporations, such as the editorial policy of the South African Broadcasting Corporation, which, with its public service mandate, ought to have no excuse for the routine exclusion of marginalised voice(s).

Encouraging the widespread adoption of listening as an organising principle for news production and for normalising inclusive media diversity broadly across the news media sphere, as opposed to witnessing it only as the exception, requires reform in every aspect of the news media ecology. There is no one-size-fits-all or quick-fix solution, and it will take time. But as we have outlined throughout this book, this is an undertaking of such high value that it more than justifies the work and time it will take to achieve.

NOTES

ACKNOWLEDGEMENTS

1   We have not listed the names of the individual members of each community who participated in this project here because some of the participants requested anonymity for reasons related to their personal safety.

CHAPTER 3

1   This refers to the practice, which has historically been a small but integral part of hostel life, of powerful officials and individuals and/or organised groups offering rooms or a bed within a room, for monetary compensation.
2   In 2008, after an intensive and factional power struggle within the ruling ANC, the sitting president of the country, Thabo Mbeki, was recalled from his position by the ANC's National Executive Committee. The leader of the faction that was behind this recall was Jacob Zuma, who then became the new president of the country after the 2009 general elections.
3   Since this interview took place in August 2017, two Glebelands residents have been convicted of murder. These came after years of false starts, delays, 'lost' evidence and general obstruction on the part of the police, and also after years of community testimony, mobilisation and pressure.

CHAPTER 5

1   Dolomite is a type of rock that has cavities or cracks in it; it slowly changes into soil when exposed to sun, wind and rain. When rain water runs into the cracks in dolomite rock, it dissolves the rock causing it to disintegrate. A sinkhole is formed when the layer of soil that covers the dolomite rock collapses.
2   Sun City is the popular name for the main prison in Johannesburg; its formal name is the Johannesburg Correctional Services Centre.

3   He was shot in the mouth and was taken to hospital by the protestors. As a result of the shooting, Miya permanently lost several teeth. Even though he opened a case against the police for the shooting, nothing ever came of it.

CHAPTER 6

1   As quoted in Joseph (2015). Blikkiesdorp is a tin shack settlement located about 25 kilometres from the Cape Town CBD, near the international airport. Initially meant to be a 'temporary relocation area', it has become home for up to 2000 households for the last ten years.

2   *The Shore Break* covers the community's struggles against both the N2 toll road and the mining project, with ACC leader and activist Nonhle Mbuthuma at the centre. The documentary was widely distributed and seen throughout South Africa and globally in 2015 and has received numerous awards. See www. theshorebreakmovie.com.

CHAPTER 7

1   For purposes of this discussion and analysis, it should be noted that the use of the term 'elites' is more descriptive of those who are part of the ruling class as opposed to a specific and organised collection of social and intellectual forces who possess and exercise the most power in society but who do not have direct control over the means of material and intellectual production; that is, as part of 'elitist theory' as propounded by, among others, Pareto (1935), Mosca (1939) and Wright Mills (1956).

CHAPTER 10

1   See, for example, Back (2007); Berger (2003); Bickford (1996); Couldry (2009, 2010); Dreher (2017); Duncan (2012); Friedman (2011); Garman and Malila (2017); Malila (2013, 2014, 2017); Malila and Garman (2016); Reid (2012); Wasserman (2013, 2017); Wasserman, Bosch and Chuma (2018); Wasserman, Chuma and Bosch (2016).

BIBLIOGRAPHY

Abrahams, Luci and Kiru Pillay. 2014. The Lived Cost of Communications: Experiencing the Lived Cost of Mobile Communications in Low and Very Low Income Households in Urban South Africa 2014. R2K and LINK Centre Research Project. http://pmg-assets.s3-website-eu-west-1.amazonaws.com/160921R2K-lived-cost-communications.pdf (accessed 3 October 2018).

ANC (African National Congress). 2012. 53rd ANC National Conference Resolutions, December, Mangaung. *South African History Online.* https://www.sahistory.org.za/archive/53rd-anc-national-conference-resolutions-december-2012 (accessed 3 October 2018).

Alexander, Peter. 2010. Rebellion of the Poor: South Africa's Service Delivery Protests – A Preliminary Analysis. *Review of African Political Economy* 37(123): 25–40. https://doi.org/10.1080/03056241003637870.

Alexander, Peter, Thapelo Lekgowa, Botsang Mmope, Luke Sinwell and Bongani Xezwi. 2012. *Marikana: A View from the Mountain and a Case to Answer.* Johannesburg: Jacana Media.

Angelopulo, George and Petrus Potgieter. 2020. The Access to the News Media by Selected Segments of the South African Population. Forthcoming by the Media Policy and Democracy Project.

Back, Les. 2007. *The Art of Listening.* Oxford: Berg.

Ballard, Richard, Adam Habib and Imraan Valodia, eds. 2006. *Voices of Protest: Social Movements in Post-Apartheid South Africa.* Pietermaritzburg: University of KwaZulu-Natal Press.

Barthes, Roland. [1957] 1972. *Mythologies.* Translated by Annette Lavers. London: Paladin.

Berger, Guy. 2003. The Journalism of Poverty and the Poverty of Journalism. Conference paper delivered at the International Communications Forum, Cape Town, 5–9 April.

Berger, Guy. 2006. Characteristics of African Media Markets. Paper for workshop convened by Forum Media and Development, Academy Eichholz Castle, Germany, 15–16 September.

Bickford, Susan. 1996. *The Dissonance of Democracy: Listening, Conflict, and Citizenship.* Ithaca, NY and London: Cornell University Press.

Bourdieu, Pierre. 1998. The Essence of Neoliberalism. *Le Monde Diplomatique*, December. http://mondediplo.com/1998/12/08bourdieu (accessed 4 January 2019).

BCCSA (Broadcasting Complaints Commission of South Africa). 1999. BCCSA's Code of Conduct for Subscription Broadcasting Service Licensees. https://bccsa.co.za/codes-of-conduct/ (accessed 20 January 2018).

BCCSA (Broadcasting Complaints Commission of South Africa). 2009. BCCSA Free-to-Air Code of Conduct for Broadcasting Service Licensees. https://bccsa.co.za/codes-of-conduct/ (accessed 20 January 2018).

Bullock, Heather E., Karen Fraser Wyche and Wendy R. Williams. 2001. Media Images of the Poor. *Journal of Social Issues* 57(2): 229–246. http://dx.doi.org/10.1111/0022-4537.00210.

Caldwell, Marc. 2011. Between Proceduralism and Substantialism in Communication Ethics. In *Communication and Media Ethics in South Africa*, edited by Natalie Hyde-Clarke, 58–75. Cape Town: Juta.

Congress of the People. 1955. The Freedom Charter: Adopted at Kliptown, Johannesburg, on June 25 and 26, 1955. http://www.historicalpapers.wits.ac.za/inventories/inv_pdfo/AD1137/AD1137-Ea6-1-001-jpeg.pdf (accessed 10 January 2018).

Couldry, Nick. 2009. Rethinking the Politics of Voice. *Continuum: Journal of Media and Cultural Studies* 23(4): 579–582. https://doi.org/10.1080/10304310903026594.

Couldry, Nick. 2010. *Why Voice Matters: Culture and Politics after Neoliberalism*. London: Sage.

De Haas, Mary. 2016. The Killing Fields of KZN: Local Government Elections, Violence and Democracy in 2016. *South African Crime Quarterly* 57: 43–53. http://dx.doi.org/10.17159/2413-3108/2016/v0n57a456.

Dreher, Tanja. 2009. Listening across Difference: Media and Multiculturalism beyond the Politics of Voice. *Continuum: Journal of Media and Cultural Studies* 23(4): 445–458. https://doi.org/10.1080/10304310903015712.

Dreher, Tanja. 2017. Listening: A Normative Approach to Transform Media and Democracy. In *Media and Citizenship: Between Marginalisation and Participation*, edited by Anthea Garman and Herman Wasserman, 16–34. Cape Town: HSRC Press.

Duncan, Jane. 2009. The Uses and Abuses of Political Economy: The ANC's Media Policy. *Transformation: Critical Perspectives on Southern Africa* 70: 1–30. doi:10.1353/trn.0.0039.

Duncan, Jane. 2012. SABC: Marikana and the Problem of Pack Journalism. *Abahlali baseMjondolo*, 11 October. http://abahlali.org/node/9253 (accessed 7 October 2019).

Duncan, Jane. 2013a. South African Journalism and the Marikana Massacre: A Case Study of an Editorial Failure. *Political Economy of Communication* 1(2): 65–88.

Duncan, Jane. 2013b. Downsizing Press Transformation. *South African Civil Society Information Service*. http://sacsis.org.za/site/article/1804 (accessed 3 August 2018).

Duncan Jane. 2015. Pluralism with Little Diversity: The South African Experience of Media Transformation. In *Media Pluralism and Diversity*, edited by Peggy Valcke, Miklos Sükösd and Robert Picard. London: Palgrave Macmillan.

Duncan, Jane. 2016. *Protest Nation: The Right to Protest in South Africa*. Pietermaritzburg: University of KwaZulu-Natal Press.

Duncan, Jane and Julie Reid. 2013. Toward a Measurement Tool for the Monitoring of Media Diversity and Pluralism in South Africa: A Public-centred Approach. *Communicatio: South African Journal for Communication Theory and Research* 39(4): 483–500. https://doi.org/10.1080/02500167.2013.864448.

Encyclopaedia Britannica. 2017. Pondoland. https://www.britannica.com/place/Pondoland (accessed 4 January 2018).

Ford, Liz. 2019. Not One Single Country Set to Achieve Gender Equality by 2030. *The Guardian*, 3 June. https://www.theguardian.com/global-development/2019/jun/03/not-one-single-country-set-to-achieve-gender-equality-by-2030 (accessed 6 June 2019).

Friedman, Steven. 2011. Whose Freedom? South Africa's Press, Middle-class Bias and the Threat of Control. *Equid Novi: African Journalism Studies* 32(2): 106–121. https://doi.org/10.1080/02560054.2011.578887.

Garman, Anthea and Vanessa Malila. 2017. Listening and the Ambiguities of Voice in South African Journalism. *Communicatio: South African Journal for Communication Theory and Research* 43(1): 1–16. https://doi.org/10.1080/02500167.2016.1226914.

Garman, Anthea and Herman Wasserman. 2017. *Media and Citizenship: Between Marginalisation and Participation*. Cape Town: HSRC Press.

George, Susan. 1997. How to Win the War of Ideas: Lessons from the Gramscian Right. *Dissent* (Summer): 47–53.

Gift of the Givers/Ubunye. 2015. Gift of the Givers Goes to Glebelands. Press release, 9 October.

Glebelands Hostel Community Violence Victims. 2016a. Invitation. Glebelands hostel community crisis press conference, Durban.

Glebelands Hostel Community Violence Victims. 2016b. Press Release. Glebelands hostel community crisis press conference, Durban.

Glebelands Hostel Community Violence Victims. 2016c. Press Release: ANN7 Apologises to the Glebelands Hostel Community Violence Victims! A Victory for Community Struggle! Durban.

Gramsci, Antonio. 1971. *Selections from Prison Notebooks*, edited by Quinton Hoare. London: Lawrence and Wishart.

Hall, Stuart. 1980. Encoding/Decoding. In *Culture, Media, Language*, edited by Stuart Hall, Dorothy Hobson, Andrew Lowe and Paul Willis, 128–138. London: Hutchinson.

Heleta, Savo. 2016. Academics Can Change the World – If They Stop Talking Only to Their Peers. *The Conversation*, 9 March. http://theconversation.com/academics-can-change-the-world-if-they-stop-talking-only-to-their-peers-55713 (accessed 5 June 2019).

Herman, Edward and Noam Chomsky. 1988. Conclusions. Excerpted from *Manufacturing Consent: The Political Economy of the Mass Media*. https://chomsky.info/consent02/ (accessed 8 January 2018).

Himmelstein, Daniel S., Ariel R. Romero, Jacob G. Levernier, Thomas A. Munro, Stephen R. McLaughlin, Bastian G. Tzovaras and Casey S. Greene. 2017. Sci-Hub Provides Access to Nearly All Scholarly Literature. *PeerJ*, 20 July. https://peerj.com/preprints/3100v1/ (accessed 17 August 2017).

Husband, Charles. 1996. The Right to be Understood: Conceiving the Multi-ethnic Public Sphere. *Innovation: The European Journal of Social Sciences* 9(2): 205–215. https://doi.org/10.1080/13511610.1996.9968484.

Husband, Charles. 2008. Listening and Understanding. Paper presented at the seminar of the Listening Project, University of Technology, Sydney, 13 November.

IEC (Independent Electoral Commission). 2016a. 2016 Municipal Election Results Summary. http://www.elections.org.za/content/LGEPublicReports/402/Detailed%20Results/GP/JHB.pdf (last modified 11 August 2016).

IEC (Independent Electoral Commission). 2016b. 2016 Municipal Elections Leaderboard. https://www.elections.org.za/lgedashboard2016/leaderboard.aspx (last modified 11 August 2016).

Jones, Harrison. 2016. Journalism's Lack of Diversity Threatens its Long term Future. *The Guardian*, 4 August. https://www.theguardian.com/media/2016/aug/04/journalism-diversity-newspapers (accessed 20 January 2018).

Joseph, Raymond. 2015. South Africans Voice Anger at Country's Media Environment. *Xindex*, 26 November. https://www.indexoncensorship.org/2015/11/ray-joseph-south-africans-voice-anger-at-countrys-media-environment/ (accessed 4 February 2019).

Kapralos, Krista. 2018. Why Local Journalism Makes a Difference. *Nieman Reports*, 14 June. http://niemanreports.org/articles/keeping-journalism-local/ (accessed 15 December 2018).

Karppinen, Kari. 2007. Making a Difference to Media Pluralism: A Critique of the Pluralistic Consensus in European Media Policy. In *Reclaiming the Media: Communication Rights and Democratic Media Roles*, edited by B. Cammaerts and N. Carpentier, 9–30. Bristol: Intellect Books.

Lee, Harper. 1960. *To Kill a Mockingbird*. Philadelphia: J.B. Lippincott & Co. Lipari, Lisbeth. 2010. Listening, Thinking, Being. *Communication Theory* 20(3): 348–362. https://doi.org/10.1111/j.1468-2885.2010.01366.x.

Lyons, Kate. 2018. 'Zero Shame': Politics Live Editor Defends All-female Line-up on New BBC Show. *The Guardian*, 4 September. https://www.theguardian.com/media/2018/sep/04/zero-shame-editor-defends-all-female-line-up-on-new-bbc-politics-show (accessed 4 September 2018).

Macnamara, Jim. 2012. Beyond Voice: Audience-making and the Work and Architecture of Listening as New Media Literacies. *Continuum: Journal of Media and Cultural Studies* 27(1): 160–175. https://doi.org/10.1080/10304312.2013.736950.

Madlala, Cyril. 2016. Death Stalks Glebelands: Plea to UN to Stop the Hostel Killings. *Daily Maverick*, 20 April. http://www.dailymaverick.co.za/article/2016-04-20-death-stalks-glebelands-plea-to-un-to-stop-the-hostel-killings/#.Vx5JN41unIU (accessed 11 November 2016).

Malila, Vanessa, comp. 2013. A Baseline Study of Youth Identity, the Media and Public Sphere in South Africa. Report, School of Journalism and Media Studies, Rhodes University. https://www.academia.edu/31191404/A_baseline_study_of_youth_identity_the_media_and_the_public_sphere_in_South_Africa (accessed 11 January 2015).

Malila, Vanessa. 2014. The Voiceless Generation – (Non-)representations of Young Citizens in the Coverage of Education Stories by South African Newspapers. *Communicare* 33(1): 21–34. https://hdl.handle.net/10520/EJC156802.

Malila, Vanessa. 2017. We Are Not the 'Born Frees': The Real Political and Civic Lives of Eight Young South Africans. In *Media and Citizenship: Between Marginalisation and Participation*, edited by Anthea Garman and Herman Wasserman, 217–232. Cape Town: HSRC Press.

Malila, Vanessa and Anthea Garman. 2016. Listening to the 'Born Frees': Politics and Disillusionment in South Africa. *African Journalism Studies* 37(1): 64–80. https://doi.org/10.1080/23743670.2015.1084587.

Marais, Hein. 1998. *South Africa: Limits to Change: The Political Economy of Transformation*. London: Zed Books.

Marinovich, Greg. 2012. The Murder Fields of Marikana: The Cold Murder Fields of Marikana. *Daily Maverick*, 8 September. https://www.dailymaverick.co.za/article/2012-09-08-the-murder-fields-of-marikana-the-cold-murder-fields-of-marikana/ (accessed 20 November 2018).

Marx, Karl and Friedrich Engels. [1947] 1970. *The German Ideology*, edited by Christopher J. Arthur. New York: International Publishers.

Mbeki, Govan. 1964. *The Peasants' Revolt*. London: Penguin.

McDonald, David A. 2002. The Bell Tolls for Thee: Cost Recovery, Cutoffs, and the Affordability of Municipal Services in South Africa. Special Report, Municipal Services Project. http://ccs.ukzn.ac.za/files/msp%20cos3.pdf (accessed 7 October 2019).

McKinley, Dale T. 2002. South Africa: Behind the Battle of Thembelihle. *Green Left Weekly*, 28 August, Issue 506. https://www.greenleft.org.au/content/south-africa-behind-battle-thembelihle (accessed 5 January 2019).

McKinley, Dale T. 2017. *South Africa's Corporatised Liberation: A Critical Analysis of the ANC in Power*. Johannesburg: Jacana Media.

McKinley, Dale T. and Ahmed Veriava. 2007. South Africa: Voices Cry from under New Myths about 'Ordinary' Country. *Business Day*, 1 October. https://allafrica.com/stories/200710010509.html (accessed 7 October 2019).

McKinley, Dale T. and Ahmed Veriava. 2010. *Arresting Dissent: State Repression and Post-Apartheid Social Movements*. Saarbrucken: Lambert Academic Publishing.

Mosca, Gaetano. 1939. *The Ruling Class*. London: McGraw-Hill.

Nandy, Ashis. 1983. *The Intimate Enemy: Loss and Recovery of Self under Colonialism*. Oxford: Oxford University Press.

Naidoo, Prishani and Ahmed Veriava. 2003. Re-membering Movements: Trade Unions and New Social Movements in Neoliberal South Africa. Research Report No. 28, Centre for Civil Society, University of KwaZulu-Natal, Durban. http://ccs.ukzn.ac.za/files/RReport_28.pdf (accessed 7 October 2019).

Ngomba, Teke. 2011. Journalists' Perceptions of 'the Audience' and the Logics of Participatory Development/Communication: A Contributory Note. *Ecquid Novi: African Journalism Studies* 32(1): 4–24. https://doi.org/10.1080/02560054.2011.545560.

Nkosi, Bongani. 2013. Over 50 Pupils without Schools Weeks after Academic New Year. *Mail & Guardian*, 24 January. https://mg.co.za/article/2013-01-24-school-admission-plagues-pupils-weeks-after-academic-new-year (accessed 11 June 2019).

O'Connor, Kim. 2003. Dialectic. *University of Chicago Theories of Media*. http://csmt.uchicago.edu/ glossary2004/dialectic.htm (accessed 20 July 2018).

O'Donnell, Penny. 2009. Journalism, Change and Listening Practices. *Continuum: Journal of Media and Cultural Studies* 23(4): 503–517. https://doi.org/10.1080/10304310903015720.

O'Donnell, Penny, Justine Lloyd and Tanja Dreher. 2009. Listening, Pathbuilding and Continuations: A Research Agenda for the Analysis of Listening. *Continuum: Journal of Media and Cultural Studies* 23(4): 423–439. https://doi.org/10.1080/10304310903056252.

Olalde, Mark. 2017. The Pondoland Rebellion. *Roads & Kingdoms*, 10 April. https://roadsandkingdoms.com/2017/rebellion-in-pondoland/ (accessed 4 January 2019).

Olivier, Bert. 2016. Why Capitalism Cannot Afford to Support the Human Sciences. *Mail & Guardian*, 20 December. http://thoughtleader.co.za/bertolivier/2016/12/20/why-capitalism-cannot-afford-to-support-the-human-sciences/ (accessed 17 August 2017).

Oxfam. 2014. Even It Up: Time to End Extreme Inequality. https://www.oxfam.org / sites/www.oxfam.org/files/file_attachments/cr-even-it-up-extreme-inequality-291014-en.pdf (accessed 4 January 2019).

Pareto, Vilfredo. 1935. *The Mind and Society*. London: Jonathan Cape.

Pearce, Fred. 2017. Murder in Pondoland: How a Proposed Mine Brought Conflict to South Africa. *The Guardian*, 28 March. https://www.theguardian.com/environment/2017/mar/27/murder-pondoland-how-proposed-mine-brought-conflict-south-africa-activist-sikhosiphi-rhadebe?CMP=share_btn_fb (accessed 21 September 2018).

Phala, Mbali. 2016. After Years of Protest, Thembelihle is Finally Getting Electricity. *The Daily Vox*, 30 June. https://www.thedailyvox.co.za/years-protest-thembelihle-finally-getting-electricity/ (accessed 11 June 2019).

Plaisance, Patrick L. 2009. The Concept of Media Accountability Reconsidered. *Journal of Mass Media Ethics: Exploring Questions of Media Morality* 15(4): 257–268. https://doi.org/10.1207/S15327728JMME1504_5.

Pointer, Rebecca. 2015. From Illegitimate Disruption to Failing State: How South African Newspapers Framed 'Service Delivery Protests' in 2013. Unpublished MA dissertation, University of Cape Town.

Posetti, Julie. 2018a. Informal interview conducted by Julie Reid with Julie Posetti.

Posetti, Julie. 2018b. The Year of the Fight Back: Predictions for Journalism 2019. *Niemanlab*. http://www.niemanlab.org/2018/12/the-year-of-the-fight-back/ (accessed 21 December 2018).

PCSA (Press Council of South Africa). 2016. Press Code of Ethics and Conduct for South African Print and Online Media. http://www.presscouncil.org.za/ContentPage?code=PRESSCODE (accessed 18 June 2018).

Pugliese, Stanislao. 2016. A Specter Haunting America: Trump and Italian Fascism. *La Voca di New York*, 20 November. http://www.lavocedinewyork.com/en/2016/11/20/a-specter-haunting-america-trump-and-italian-fascism/ (accessed 4 January 2019).

Reid, Julie. 2012. Media Freedom Debacles Aside, the Press is Failing Us. *Daily Maverick*, 24 October. https://www.dailymaverick.co.za/opinionista/2012-10-24-media-freedom-debacles-aside-the-press-is-failing-us/ (accessed 14 March 2017).

Reid, Julie. 2014. Third-party Complaints in the System of Press Regulation: Inviting the Reader to Take Part in Journalistic Accountability and Securing Press Freedom. *Ecquid Novi: African Journalism Studies* 35(2): 58–74. https://doi.org/10.1080/02560054.2014.919943.

Reid, Julie. 2016. Media Content Diversity in SA: Why is Government Still Asking All the Wrong Questions? *Daily Maverick*, 29 August. https://www.dailymaverick.co.za/opinionista/2016-08-29-media-content-diversity-in-sa-why-is-government-still-asking-all-the-wrong-questions/#.WJG4jxvavIU (accessed 1 February 2017).

Reid, Julie. 2017a. Counter-mythologising 'Media Freedom': Including the Audience in Media Freedom Discourses and a New Normative Position for the Global South. *Communicatio: South African Journal for Communication Theory and Research* 43(2): 74–92. https://doi.org/10.1080/02500167.2017.1337648.

Reid, Julie. 2017b. Political Myth-making in Media Policy: The Case of the African National Congress Versus the Press Council of South Africa. *Journal of African Media Studies* 9(3): 521–546. https://doi.org/10.1386/jams.9.3.521_1.

Reid, Julie. 2018a. Decolonizing Education and Research by Countering the Myths We Live by. *Cinema Journal* 57(1): 132–138.

Reid, Julie. 2018b. Presentation of the Main Findings of the UNESCO World Trends in Freedom of Expression and Media Development: Global Report 2017/2018. Unpublished conference paper delivered at the UNESCO World Press Freedom Day Conference, Accra, Ghana, 3 May.

Reid, Julie and Taryn Isaacs. 2015. Press Regulation in South Africa: An Analysis of the Press Council of South Africa, the Press Freedom Commission and Related Discourses. *The Media Policy and Democracy Project.* http://www.mediaanddemocracy.com/research-reports.html (accessed 20 January 2018).

Right2Know Campaign. 2015. Stop the Killings in Glebelands! *Right2Know Campaign*, 4 May. https://www.r2k.org.za/2015/05/04/glebelands/ (accessed 13 November 2016).

Rodny-Gumede, Ylva. 2015. Marikana Massacre: How South African Journalism Failed the Test. *Mail & Guardian*, 25 November. https://mg.co.za/article/2015-11-25-marikana-massacre-how-south-african-journalism-failed-the-test (accessed 2 January 2018).

Rusbridger, Alan. 2018. Alan Rusbridger: Who Broke the News? *The Guardian*, 31 August. https://www.theguardian.com/news/2018/aug/31/alan-rusbridger-who-broke-the-news (accessed 13 January 2019).

Sage, Lily and C.J. Polychroniou. 2016. Interview: Noam Chomsky on the Perils of Market-driven Education. *Truthout*, 22 October. http://www.truth-out.org/opinion/item/38066-noam-chomsky-on-the-perils-of-market-driven-education (accessed 17 August 2017).

SAHA (South African HIstory Archive). 1992. Political Assassinations 1974–1994. https://www.sahistory.org.za/article/political-assassinations-1974-1994 (accessed 9 October 2019).

SAHO (South African History Online). 2011. Transkei. http://www.sahistory.org.za/places/transkei (accessed 11 June 2019).

SAHO (South African History Online). 2013. Pondoland. http://www.sahistory.org.za/article/pondoland (accessed 8 January 2019).

Samalavicius, Almantas. 2016. Higher Education and Neoliberal Temptation: An Interview with Henry A. Giroux. *Eurozine*, 9 May. http://www.truth-out.org/news/item/35956-higher-education-and-neoliberal-temptation (accessed 18 January 2019).

Satgar, Vishwas. 2010. Narrowing Freedom of Expression. *Amandla!* 16: 18–19. http://aidc.org.za/amandla-media/amandla-magazine/back-issues/ (accessed 4 January 2019).

Savides, Matthew. 2016. Slain ANC Councillor Strove for Peace at Violence-wracked Glebelands Hostel. *Times Live*, 17 April. http://www.timeslive.co.za/sundaytimes/stnews/2016/04/17/Slain-ANC-councillor-strove-for-peace-at-violence-wracked-Glebelands-Hostel (accessed 11 November 2016).

Sefali, Pharie. 2015. Twenty-one Deaths in 13 Months at Glebelands Hostel. *GroundUp*, 13 March. http://www.groundup.org.za/article/twenty-one-deaths-13-months-glebelands-hostel_2757/ (accessed 11 November 2016).

Segodi, Siphiwe. 2018. The Never-ending Housing Challenge – Reflection on Thembelihle. *Daily Maverick*, 13 March. https://www.dailymaverick.co.za/article/2018-03-13-op-ed-the-never-ending-housing-challenge-reflection-on-thembelihle/#.WsiL4Lj5530 (accessed 4 February 2019).

SERI (Socio-Economic Rights Institute). 2013. Thembelihle: Engaging with an Unresponsive State. Community Practice Notes: Informal Settlement Series. http://www.seri-sa.org/images/Thembelihle_CPN_Final.pdf (accessed 8 October 2010).

Servaes, Jan and Patchanee Malikhao. 2005. Participatory Communication: The New Paradigm? In *Media & Glocal Change: Rethinking Communication for Development*, edited by Oscar Hemer and Thomas Tufte, 91–103. Buenos Aires: Nordicom and CLACSO. http://bibliotecavirtual.clacso.org.ar/ar/libros/edicion/ media/media.html (accessed 17 June 2017).

Simkins, Charles. 2014. The Distribution of Income and the Distribution of Wealth in South Africa Part 1 – The Facts. *Helen Suzman Foundation*, 1 September. http://hsf.org.za/resource-centre/hsf-briefs/the-distribution-of-income-and-the-distribution-of-wealth-in-south-africa-part-i-the-facts (accessed 4 February 2019).

StatsSA (Statistics South Africa). 2015. Methodological Report on Rebasing on National Poverty Lines and Development of Pilot Provincial Poverty Lines. http://www.statssa.gov.za/publications/Report-03-10-11/Report-03-10-11.pdf (accessed 9 January 2019).

Tacchi, Jo A. 2008. Voice and Poverty. *Media Development* 1: 1–7.

Thompson, Audrey. 2003. Listening and its Asymmetries. *Curriculum Inquiry* 33(1): 79–100. https://doi.org/10.1111/1467-873X.00251.

TRC (Truth and Reconciliation Commission). 1998. Final Report: The Pondoland Revolt. http://sabctrc.saha.org.za/reports/volume2/chapter5/subsection18.htm (accessed 9 October 2019).

Ubunye bama Hostela, Right2Know KZN, KZN Violence Monitor, South Durban Community Environmental Alliance, Democratic Left Front KZN, Community Justice Movement and Centre for Civil Society. 2014. South Africa: Police Torture at Glebelands Ends Fragile Peace. *Pambazuka News*, 9 October. https://www.pambazuka.org/human-security/south-africa-police-torture-glebelands-ends-fragile-peace (accessed 4 February 2019).

UNESCO (United Nations Educational, Scientific and Cultural Organization). 2014. World Trends in Freedom of Expression and Media Development: Global Report 2013/2014. https://unesdoc.unesco.org/ark:/48223/pf0000227025 (accessed 28 August 2018).

UNESCO (United Nations Educational, Scientific and Cultural Organization). 2018. World Trends in Freedom of Expression and Media Development: Global Report 2017/2018. https://en.unesco.org/world-media-trends-2017 (accessed 28 August 2018).

Van Cuilenburg, Jan. 2007. Media Diversity, Competition and Concentration: Concepts and Theories. In *Media between Culture and Commerce*, edited by Els de Bens, 25–54. Bristol: Intellect Books.

Viljoen, Henning. 2016. Judgment: Glebelands Hostel Community Violence Victims (South Durban KZN) vs. Multichoice Channel 404. Case Number: 14/2016. *Broadcasting Complaints Commission of South Africa*. http://bccsa.co.za/2016/09/21/case-number-142016-glebelands-hostel-community-violence-victims-south-durban-kzn-vs-multichoice-channel-404-disclosed-identities/ (accessed 9 November 2016).

Viner, Katharine. 2017. A Mission for Journalism in a Time of Crisis. *The Guardian*, 16 November. https://www.theguardian.com/news/2017/nov/16/a-mission-for-journalism-in-a-time-of-crisis (accessed 20 January 2018).

Von Holdt, Karl. 2013. South Africa: The Transition to Violent Democracy. *Review of African Political Economy* 40(138): 589–604. https://doi.org/10.1080/03056244.2013.854040.

Wasserman, Herman. 2013. Journalism in a New Democracy: The Ethics of Listening. *Communicatio: South African Journal for Communication Theory and Research* 39(1): 67–84. https://doi.org/10.1080/02500167.2013.772217.

Wasserman, Herman. 2017. South Africa's Media Should Beware of Being the Voice of Only Some. *News24*, 19 October. http://www.news24.com/Columnists/GuestColumn/south-africas-media-should-beware-of-being-the-voice-of-only-some-20171019 (accessed 20 July 2018).

Wasserman, Herman, Tanja Bosch and Wallace Chuma. 2018. Communication from Above and Below: Media, Protest and Democracy. *Politikon: South African Journal of Political Studies* 45(3): 368–386. https://doi.org/10.1080/02589346.2018.1446482.

Wasserman, Herman, Wallace Chuma and Tanja Bosch. 2016. Voices of the Poor are Missing from South Africa's Media. *University of Cape Town*, 4 March. http://www.uct.ac.za/dailynews/?id=9602 (accessed 14 March 2017).

Weale, Sally. 2016. Privately Educated Elite Continues to Take Top Jobs, Finds Survey. *The Guardian*, 24 February. https://www.theguardian.com/education/2016/feb/24/privately-educated-elite-continues-to-take-top-jobs-finds-survey (accessed 20 November 2018).

Wright Mills, Charles. 1956. *The Power Elite*. Oxford: Oxford University Press.

Wurgaft, Lewis D. 1985. Review of *The Intimate Enemy: Loss and Recovery of Self Under Colonialism* by Ashis Nandy. *Journal of Asian Studies* 44(2): 434–436. doi:10.2307/2055978.

Zulu, Paulus. 1993. Durban Hostels and Political Violence: Case Studies in KwaMashu and Umlazi. *Transformation* 21: 1–23.

Printed and bound by CPI Group (UK) Ltd, Croydon, CR0 4YY

13/04/2025

14656582-0006